The Orvis Field Guide to

Shotgun Care & Maintenance

The Orvis Field Guide Series

*The Orvis Field Guide to
Shotgun Care & Maintenance*

*The Orvis Field Guide to
First Aid for Sporting Dogs*

*The Orvis Shooting School
Method of Wingshooting*

The Orvis Field Guide to

Shotgun Care & Maintenance

by
Tom Morrow
Professional Gunsmith

In collaboration with
The ORVIS GUNSMITHING DIVISION

With photographs & illustrations by
Laurie Morrow, Series Editor

WILLOW CREEK PRESS
MINOCQUA, WISCONSIN

© 2000 by Tom Morrow and Laurie Bogart Morrow,
Freedom, New Hampshire

Text, Photographs and Illustrations
by Laurie Bogart Morrow

Published in 2000 by Willow Creek Press,
P.O. Box 147, Minocqua, Wisconsin 54548

The Orvis Field Guide Series of Wingshooting, Waterfowling,
Shotgunning and Field Dog books is the creative property of Laurie
Bogart Morrow. All rights reserved.

Cover photograph courtesy of The Orvis Company

For information on other Willow Creek titles,
call 1-800-850-WILD

Printed in Canada

Library of Congress Cataloging-in-Publication Data
Morrow, Tom
The Orvis field guide to shotgun care & maintenance / by Tom
Morrow ; in collaboration with The Orvis Gunsmithing Division ;
with photographs & illustrations by Laurie Morrow.
p. cm. -- (The Orvis field guide series)
ISBN 1-57223-316-8 (hardcover : alk. paper)
1. Shotguns—Maintenance and repair. I. Morrow, Laurie. II. Orvis
Company. Gunsmithing Division. III. Title. IV. Series.
TS536.8. M67 2000
683.4'26'0288—dc21
00-009384

In Recognition of the works of
JAMES VIRGIL HOWE,
JACK O'CONNOR, P.O. ACKLEY and
COLONEL TOWNSEND WHELEN

Whose knowledge of sporting firearms
and devotion to game and gun
helped define our sport.

DISCLAIMER

The Authors, Publisher and The Orvis Company, together or separately, shall in no way be held responsible or liable for personal injury, injury to others, damage to property or inconvenience, or be held answerable or liable for such, or for any liability of any nature that may be incurred or sustained by a person or persons as a direct or indirect result of the use, interpretation, or implementation of any part or whole of the contents of this book.

It is to be emphasized in no uncertain terms that the handling of a firearm or firearms of any type and in any manner is by the desire, decision and determination of an individual; and therefore, is at the sole discretion of that individual and in every regard entirely his or her exclusive responsibility, for which that person must and shall be held unconditionally accountable.

SHOTGUNNER'S RULE OF THUMB

IF YOU CONSIDER YOURSELF TO BE AN EXPERT and have used firearms responsibly for many years, you already have integrated the fundamental rules of gun safety into the manner in which you handle firearms. But remember the old adage, "familiarity breeds contempt." Do not be overly sure of your proficiency with gun in hand. Unchecked lapses in attention can have unexpected and potentially hazardous results. *Handling a firearm is an activity that requires constant concentration….*

IF YOU ARE A PERSON WHO IS NEW TO THE SHOOTING SPORTS, then memorize the rules and theory of gun safety until the practice becomes second nature to you. *Proceed slowly; double-check yourself until you are comfortable and confident in your ability to safely handle your gun….*

IF YOU KNOW SOMEONE WHO BELIEVES THAT RULES ARE MEANT TO BE BROKEN, then you are dealing with a careless and potentially dangerous shooter. *Keep your distance from this sort of person!*

GUN: A mechanism for exploding a charge and directing a bullet.

—JAMES VIRGIL HOWE

FOREWORD

WE WHO SHOULDER A SHOTGUN OR CAST A FLY are a singular bunch, for in the realm of the outdoors, we enthusiasts tend to embrace our sport with a passion that lasts a lifetime. You know or have read of the old hunter, the old angler, but you rarely hear about the old downhill racer or septuagenarian paraglider. We are content, even and most especially in our dotage, to sit alongside a tranquil trout stream and pitch a Royal Coachman into a dark and promising pool. And when we hunt alongside the son of the son of our first setter, we retrace our footsteps and memories to the very same secret grouse covert we have visited unfailingly for each of countless seasons. In the rustling of the autumn woods, we hear a voice whisper from somewhere inside, like the call of a crusader to a pilgrimage. There is, after all, something otherworldly about the outdoor world; something wild, something awesome, something transcendent that fixes into a corner of one's soul.

Then there's the practical side and the dozens of things we get caught up with—shotgun fit, honing our techniques, picking places to hunt or shoot, choosing our guns, dogs, clothes and so on. Somewhere, usually at the bottom of the list, is the task of caring for your gun. Yet this should top the list. Surprisingly little has been written about gun care and maintenance. There are chapters in some few books and occasional magazine articles, but to my knowledge, only a handful of books have ever been dedicated to the subject, and these are long out-of-print. Consider that a gun is not just sporting equipment but a complex, mechanical tool. Suddenly the words *care* and *maintenance* take on a new meaning. A gun in less that 100-percent working order will work less than 100-percent for you. That may mean the difference between a clean kill and a crippled bird, or cost you a much-needed point during a sporting clays tournament. A gun with a fouled bore cannot work to the best of its capability; a gun that is caked with hardened oil may not work at all. A gun is not made for a season or a year; it is made for the seasons of your sporting lifetime. Given proper care, it will.

And so, the purpose of this book is to tell you how you can buy into that sort of guarantee. Because a gun is the means by which you, the shooting sportsman, embrace the great outdoors.

—LAURIE MORROW, Series Editor

CONTENTS

PREFACE

IT WAS THE FIND of a lifetime—a pigeon gun made for Captain A. H. Bogardus, the eminent 19th century wingshooter and white-wing champion, by the renowned gunmaker, W & C Scott. The handsome side-by-side had all the right bells and whistles, and superb condition, to boot—until I turned the gun over in may hands. Here was one of the most tragic victims of improper gun storage I had ever seen. Left in its elegant leather case for untold years, the unscrupulous culprit of gunmetal, rust, had blossomed from the oil-soaked case lining and virtually eaten up all of the fine English rose and scroll engraving on the left side of the receiver, now a defaced mass of festering steel. What should have been a highly desirable and extremely valuable gun was now nothing more than another "roach."

Sadly, stories like this are all too common. Improper gun storage and lack of maintenance is the single biggest casualty of firearms—not overuse, or even abuse. Just plain and simple neglect. Unfortunately, much of what comes to us professional gunsmiths is innocent damage that could easily have been prevented had the gun owner simply known better. This guidebook is meant to prevent you from falling into that boat, and to help you insure that your gun will give you a lifetime of reliable use.

To begin, we need to start at the very beginning—with gun safety.

Chapter One

HANDLING & CARING FOR FIREARMS SAFELY

NO MATTER HOW EXPERIENCED a shooter you may be, never assume at any time that a gun is safe. *You must presume a gun is unsafe until you check it carefully and thoroughly.* Then, and only then, is a gun ready to handle—and even so, you must constantly and consistently practice the rules of gun safety *at all times.*

The rules of gun safety apply particularly to the cleaning of your gun. We are cautious with our guns in the woods, on the marsh and at the range. We must be equally attentive at the workbench or in the gun room. A live cartridge in a chamber knows no distinction between the field and the gun cradle, and all that stands between security and disaster is a cocked hammer.

Perform the following procedures faithfully and adopt these recommendations when cleaning your gun, as they will insure your safety, the safety of others and the functional well-being and longevity of your firearm.

1. *Extract cartridges from the gun before cleaning. Never* work on a gun unless it is fully unloaded. Break open your double gun to make sure there are no cartridges in the breech. Open your slide-action or semi-automatic shotgun and insure that the chamber is empty; turn it upside down and make *doubly* sure that the magazine contains no live shells. *This is especially important with any gun that has a tubular magazine.* If you place snap caps in

the gun when it is not in use, double-check to be certain they are, in fact, snap caps and not live loads, as some snap caps are remarkably similar in appearance to unfired cartridges.

2. *Never shoot out a load if there is any possibility whatsoever of a bore obstruction or if there is a dent, bulge or other damage to the barrel.* Shooting out a bore obstruction or shooting a gun with damaged barrels is dangerous and has the potential to be fatal. It is most assuredly an accident waiting to happen! Please refer to "Bore Obstructions" on page 115, where the subject is covered in depth.

3. *Do not attempt to load, shoot, or clean an unfamiliar older gun unless it is first examined and deemed safe by a professional gunsmith.* "Do not

spend a moment on a firearm which is to be actually used that is not substantial, correctly designed and made, and capable of being restored to its needed strength and utility. *Never* say 'good enough' in firearms. If you can't say 'right,' put the gun in the antique cabinet, or, if broken, in the junk pile," cautioned master gunsmith and ballistics expert James V. Howe in his classic work, *The Modern Gunsmith* [Funk & Wagnalls, 1934].

I remember one "Twelfth," opening day of grouse season in Scotland, when a local farmer joined our shooting party sporting an ancient hammer gun of indiscriminate birth. It had a ruptured Damascus barrel, a missing hammer, and the cracked wrist was reinforced with wire. It probably never saw the inside of a proof house and the fellow was shooting nitro loads through it, maintaining, "If it was good enough for Grand-dad, it's good enough for me." Granted, this is an extreme case, but all of us, at some time or other, have come upon an appealing older gun that cries out to be returned to the field, especially if it has family or other sentimental attachments. Pocket your feelings and take a cold, hard look at the functional reliability of your firearm. No matter how handsome the wood grain or exquisitely engraved the action, *cosmetics in no way reflect the intrinsic mechanical reliability of the working parts of a gun.* This particularly applies to vintage Damascus-barreled guns and many pre-World War I American, British and continental fluid steel barreled guns. In the early 20th century, modern metallurgy was in its infancy. Back then, there were only a few high-carbon steels and these were elementary in composition. Chrome-moly, vanadium and other stronger, tougher barrel steels used today had yet to be refined.

Even a gun that has seen conscientious use and regular care over the years is not immune to the ravages of time and use, which can—*and do*—compromise a gun's efficiency and reliability. After excessive use or abuse, a shotgun can become off-face or develop a faulty locking mechanism. If a barrel has been reamed repeatedly or over-lapped, the barrel wall thickness can be seriously compromised and may no longer withstand the pressure of firing. *Always* check barrel wall thickness, especially in an older double gun, as lapping may have been part of its annual maintenance. A barrel should be lapped by your gunsmith *only,* and on an as needed basis.

These are just a few of any number of problems that frequently crop up in older or previously owned guns. Again, always remember: *A gun must be judged solely on its essential soundness.* There is no point renovating, taking the risk of shooting, or even cleaning a gun that mechanically and physically does not pass muster. Do so, and you will find trouble.

4. *Never Dry-Fire a Gun.* Dry-fire a double gun and you might hear the tip of the firing pin crack off. This is serious damage that will necessitate a costly professional repair—a minimum of several hundred dollars in a field-grade double, and many times more for a high-grade gun. Keep snap caps in a gun when it is not in use. Should it get into thoughtless hands, no damage will be done.

The same caution applies to an autoloader, gas, bolt-action or pump gun. You can "peen" or otherwise distort the metal around the firing pin hole. The firing pin will stick—and then the gun can no longer function properly. Never dry-fire any gun without a snap cap in the barrel.

5. *Do not disassemble or attempt to work on any gun with tools.* Leave this to the professional gunsmith. You may field strip a shotgun, if you know how, for the purposes of cleaning only. We cover certain procedures, such as tightening screws correctly and removing choke tubes, which you certainly can do. But the mechanical aspect of working on a shotgun is a complex operation that requires specific and varied knowledge, and is almost always best left to a professional gunsmith. *Different kinds of shotguns*

function differently. A side-by-side is distinct from an over/under, as is a sidelock from a boxlock. An autoloader has no bearing on the design of a slide-action. And a recoil-operated autoloader functions differently from an inertia recoil or gas-operated autoloader.

Here is a recipe for gun disaster: *A splash of unquenchable curiosity mixed with a dash of over-confidence, stirred with a hardware store screwdriver.* Nine times out of ten, the person that fits that description will end up on his gunsmith's doorstep with his hat—and gun—in his hand. *Don't* tinker with your gun's working parts.

If cleaning and caring for your gun on a regular basis is like preventative medicine, then professional cleaning and yearly maintenance is like an annual physical exam. You can practice

Removing an innocent looking screw can unwittingly open a can of worms that ultimately will lead you to your gunsmith's door.

preventative medicine on your gun—this book tells you how. But a thorough cleaning requires taking apart a gun—a complex affair even for a professional gunsmith.

For instance, working on a sidelock shotgun should always be left to the professional gunsmith (preferably a gunsmith who specializes in fine shotguns). As for semi-automatics, some gunsmiths will not even touch them because they can be very temperamental.

Here are a few examples of things that can go wrong if you are unfamiliar with the workings of your shotgun and get overzealous cleaning it….

You may remove an innocent-looking screw that inadvertently opens a can of worms and ultimately leads you to your gunsmith's door (and a costly repair). Unbeknownst to you, it may be the screw that holds a hammer in place, as in some boxlock shotguns, like those built by Parker Brothers. If this screw is removed, the mainspring is immediately released and the gun cannot be reassembled unless it is taken entirely apart—definitely a professional gunsmith's job.

In the design of the Winchester Model 12, a certain screw in the trigger group has a left-handed thread. If you insist on turning it to the right, you will strip it—and the gun will no longer work.

If you screw in the tang screw of a side-by-side shotgun too far, it will make it impossible for the safety to work.

If you remove the metal parts from a gunstock and attempt to sand the wood for any reason, chances are you will round the edges and ruin the wood-to-metal fit—irreparable damage that may necessitate a replacement stock to make the gun "right" again. A restocked, refinished, "as new" gun is worth comparatively less than the same model in good, all-original condition.

Therefore, do not meddle with the working parts of your gun. Give it regular care and maintenance to keep it working at its most efficient. That's your job. Leave the rest to your gunsmith.

6. *Only shoot loads appropriate to the gun.* There is no compromise on this point. Memorize James Virgil Howe's *unbreakable* rule: "Remember that the dividing line between black and smokeless powders is a deadline, and marks an abrupt transition in the design and make of firearms. *Never* compromise this deadline."

The "deadline" that Howe specifically mentions

"Remember that the dividing line between black and smokeless powders is a deadline, and marks an abrupt transition in the design and make of firearms. Never compromise this deadline."

– James Virgil Howe

is the transition in firearms manufacture from Damascus-barreled guns to fluid steel-barreled guns. The attractive patterns created by the browned and twisted steel of Damascus barrels camouflage a ballistically low-pressure bore appropriate only for blackpowder loads. Damascus gun production generally ceased around 1900. Fluid steel was developed to withstand the increased pressure generated by smokeless loads, and remains the technology we use for manufacture of gun barrels, albeit with ongoing improvements in metallurgy. Always take care that the load you shoot is the load the gun was designed to fire. Shooting improper loads through a gun can be harmful—or even fatal.

7. *Do not stand the gun on its butt or muzzle in an unsupported manner.* It is not uncommon for a

person to make the mistake of setting a gun casually alongside his workbench or table, only to look on helplessly as it crashes to the floor. An unsupported gun can easily fall over and almost always seems to do so in the blink of an eye. A fall can dent the barrels, nick the wood, or scratch the stock finish. If a gun crashes onto a cement floor, the fall can crack the stock at the wrist. If reparable (some wrist breaks are not), the repair involves reinforcement with dowels, recheckering and complete stock refinishing. A damaged forend can be even more complicated, and cost as much *or more* than repairing a buttstock.

It has become increasingly difficult and sometimes impossible to find a replacement buttstock or forend for an older model gun. Obtaining replacement parts—even for production guns manufactured in the *millions*, such as the Winchester Model 12—may pose a problem that will only exacerbate with time. (Fortunately, companies like Brownells, Galazan and others do maintain a good inventory of replacement parts for certain popular models.) A replacement forend or buttstock for currently manufactured guns is usually obtainable but may take a long time to get, particularly if the gun is an import. If the supplier quotes six weeks, count on twelve—then say goodbye to bird season because it will be over by the time you get your gun back. This is more the rule than the exception. That's why we gunsmiths always advise our clients to send us their guns for repair or refurbishment immediately after season is over. That way there's ample time to get them ready for the next season.

8. *Regular care and a light touch will insure the lifetime of your gun.* Over-oiling or lubricating your gun can do more damage than you may realize. Therefore, always observe the unspoken *Golden Rule of Gun Care*: Use gun oil and gun grease sparingly but thoroughly and only *after* you have first removed hardened buildup and residue.

Oil usually accumulates in tight, hard-to-get-at places, such as around the extractor, hammer, sears, and in and between other working parts. It can soak into the wood and destroy a stock's tensile strength. Excess grease or oil in the action, barrel, or chamber can impair the functioning of a shotgun's working parts. Hardened build-up can cause a shotgun to fail to cock, make the action stiff and difficult to open and, in extreme cases, even cause a shotgun to fire *when closed*.

Some years ago, I purchased a well-used BSA side-by-side, 12-gauge boxlock shotgun that was made between the world wars. It had so much hardened grease on the hammers that one of them refused to cock. If the gun had been vigorously snapped closed, the firing pin would have contacted the primer of the cartridge and quite possibly caused the gun to fire. Being a professional gunsmith, I disassembled the gun and performed a complete cleaning that cured the problem and gave me a serviceable gun, which was otherwise in excellent condition. If your gun suffers from oil build-up, give it to your gunsmith before you even attempt to pull a trigger. He will give it a thorough cleaning and check to be sure that the gun is mechanically safe and functioning properly. It is a good idea to have your gunsmith clean and check

You can't go wrong if you abide by this simple rule: Clean your gun thoroughly and oil sparingly.

your gun before you put it away after hunting or shooting season *every year*, no matter how much you have used it. Remember, age and improper storage are formidable culprits that can be as hard on your gun as extensive use, abuse, or the ravages of Nature.

9. In *The Complete Book of Rifles and Shotguns* [Harper & Row, 1961], Jack O'Connor wrote, "Most gun owners either ruin their firearms by neglect or kill them with kindness." The point made by this legendary sportsman is as true today as it was when the ink was still wet on his manuscript. On one hand, there is the person who tosses his gun without a care (or a case) into the back of his pickup truck, fires thousands of rounds through the barrel without a cleaning, and

eventually shoots out the bore. In all likelihood, this fellow bought the gun new for relatively little money and possesses the philosophy that a gun is to be used to the point of no return, after which it becomes a throwaway. We see this happen most often with standard-grade waterfowl guns, which generally are considered (and treated like) a poor cousin to classic game guns because they are subjected to heavy use in extreme conditions.

For this reason, it is unusual to find a duck gun that boasts a flame-grained walnut stock and delicate hand engraving on the action. More likely today, a new 12-gauge waterfowler features a synthetic stock trimmed out in camouflage—lock, stock and barrel. The duck hunter who is apt to shoot many loads through his gun, carry it in inclement weather over punishing terrain, and subject it to rust-loving saltwater *must* be sure he thoroughly cleans his gun after use, inside and out, or its functional lifetime will be very short indeed.

Time and again, we come across previously owned firearms that are sorely neglected. Next time you go to a sporting goods store, look around. You may be surprised at a "roach" that is squirreled away in some dark corner. Early Parker Trojans, pre-1964 Winchester Model 12s, Remington Model 11s, and innumerable unmarked continental guild guns were $20 shotguns when new.

Today, one can be worth vastly more *if* the gun has retained significant original condition (80 percent is considered the minimum standard set by collectible firearms enthusiasts). In older guns, negligence and improper storage are the primary culprits that can turn a vintage or classic model gun into a roach or "attic" gun. Have a professional gunsmith check the gun over before you even fire a round through it. *I cannot repeat this too often.* The gun may pass muster—and then again, it may not. An older gun that has had many rounds fired through it, along with regular passes of a bore brush, can *still* have years of field life remaining. But your gunsmith—not you—should be the judge of that.

Then there is the sometime-shooter who purchases a costly custom gun. Three or four times a year, the gun sees the field, the range, or the light of day. It is used as a status symbol instead of for the purpose for which it was made, as even a high-grade gun is field equipment. The owner inevitably will profusely over-oil the shotgun before tucking it away in its flannel-lined case. Months later, when it

is finally taken out again, the owner cannot under-
stand why impressions of his own fingerprints have
marred the case colors on the receiver and the once-
flawless barrel bluing (or "blacking," as the British
call it). The flannel case lining is stained by seepage
from the action, which was over-oiled before the
gun was put away. The fabric has acted like a
sponge, causing the oil to soak into the wrist of the
stock. This, in turn, has softened the sharpness of
the fine, flat-point checkering, which will quickly
wear off. Whenever oil soaks into the stock, it can
result in a "dotey" condition, which means the
wood becomes soft and easily compressed. During
the gun's long, untended hibernation, the oil-
soaked flannel lining dried, stuck to the gunmetal,
and caused rust. Every nook and cranny of the
action is packed with hardened oil. The gun will

need to be refinished and reblued. This will diminish its value, even after it has been restored to "as new" condition. That's because *any* gun in original condition bears the imprint of its maker, especially fine-finished guns with hand-rubbed oil stocks, niter or rust blueing, case colors, and engraving. A refinished gun, whether custom or factory, no longer bears the distinguishing characteristics of the original gunmaker. Because of utter carelessness, many a firearm has been demoted (and devalued) to the level of a refinished gun. Is this killing a gun with kindness? You bet it is.

Therefore, *never* over-lubricate a gun. Always wipe down the barrel and gunmetal with a damp cloth after handling to remove fingerprints. Oil *will not* remove fingerprints. Marks left by fingerprints on gunmetal are *not* from perspiration, but from salt that remains *after* perspiration has evaporated. Salt is a major cause of rust. *Only water removes salt.*

However, water in its vapor form, *moisture*, can virtually destroy a gun. Moisture is the breeding ground for rust. Rust eats gunmetal. It will mar blueing and case colors, pit a bore, roughen a chamber, and in the worst case scenario, freeze the working parts of a gun and render it utterly and permanently useless. Light rust can be removed, a bore can be lapped, and gunmetal reblued. However, in the majority of cases, rust leaves its mark, no matter how hard you try to conceal it.

Moisture comes from condensation that results when a cold gun is brought into a warm place, and from the mist or fog that rolls across the hills, a bog, marsh, or on offshore sea breezes. Moisture-laden air is humidity in hot climes. And, like the postman, moisture endures through sleet, snow or freezing rain. Water in any form—and saltwater, especially—can ruin your gun if the gun is not wiped down completely with a damp rag, and then oiled immediately. If a gun is submerged in water, wipe it down as best as you can and use a moisture displacing lubricant to lift out moisture. If the gun has been submerged in saltwater, or you are concerned that it is not thoroughly dry in the deeper working parts, bring it to your gunsmith. He will strip it and give it a professional cleaning. Remember, even a little saltwater on a mainspring will cause rust and disable a gun from working in very short order.

Rust will start within 24 hours of contact on gunmetal and a tenth of that time if the gun is exposed to saltwater. If you are shooting a couple of miles from the ocean, salt carries on the air and will likely affect your gun.

A gun stored in a gun vault is also not safe from moisture. Moisture sneaks in whenever the door of a vault is opened. Moisture hides in obscure places, such as a butt pad, leather gun sling, even gunstock wood. Although a wood blank should be thoroughly dried before it is shaped into a gunstock, wood grain always retains a degree of moisture. You commonly see on inexpensive guns that the wood-to-metal fit appears to have shrunk or, in some cases, the stock appears to be warped. This is because the blank was not completely kiln or air dried before it was shaped into a stock. For this reason, a gun—especially a gun in storage— must be wiped down on a regular basis.

NOTE: There is a clever device called a Goldenrod, available through Brownells, which circulates air and eliminates dampness, or Brownells Desi Pak® absorbs airborne moisture.

10. *After you clean your gun, always check to be sure you have not left a cleaning patch in the bore.* A patch can easily slip off a cleaning rod and lodge inconspicuously in the bore. If so, and the gun is fired, the damage can be staggering. That innocent patch is now an obstruction. The obstruction will block and arrest gases caused by the exploding charge. With nowhere to go, the gas will expand within the space in which it has been confined. The result is a barrel bulge or burst barrel. You and/or someone next to you can also get hurt. And your gun, at the very least, will need a new or

replacement barrel—if you can find or afford one. This is a serious and important topic, which is covered in detail later.

*   *   *

Follow these ten points and you will keep your gun in top working condition and ever at the ready, while at the same time insuring your personal safety and the safety of others.

Now, before we get into gun cleaning procedures, let's take a look at what you'll need to properly clean your gun. First, you need a place. Then you need the tools and materials to do the job—and do it well.

The room in which you clean your gun has to meet a number of requirements—even if you own just one gun—because you will be working with dangerous solvents.

Chapter Two

YOUR GUN ROOM

THE ROOM WHERE YOU CLEAN and care for your gun should be used primarily for that purpose. It should *not* be your kitchen or other family living area, and most emphatically *not a room that is in any way whatsoever accessible to small children or inquisitive juveniles*. You will be working with solvents that are harmful, flammable, poisonous and, if ingested, potentially fatal. If a child, or anyone else, swallows a solvent or gets aerosol sprayed in his eyes, follow the directions on the can and call 911 *immediately*. Your gun room can be in your basement, attic, a spare room or your garage. The room in which you work, however, should meet the following requirements:

1. *Your gun room door must have a secure locking arrangement, such as a strong, tamperproof lock that cannot be opened by small hands—or any hands, for that matter.* Only you and trusted adults in the household should have access to the key or know the combination. Keep the key in a secure place— *not* hanging on the key rack in the kitchen, within a child's grasp.

2. *Your gun room must be well-ventilated, with good windows or, at the very least, a door that opens to the outside.* An exhaust fan that vents out of an exterior wall is desirable, but any fan that effectively moves air and fumes to the outside is okay, providing it does the job well. Solvents give off dangerous fumes that can cause damage to your eyes, nose, skin and lungs.

3. *The room should have consistent, household-type heat during the cold months.* Any heat source with an open flame, such as a fireplace, open-faced wood or coal burning stove, kerosene camp stove, etc., is *strongly inadvisable* in the presence of solvents, which are dangerously flammable. For this reason, it is imperative that you equip your gun room with at least one fire extinguisher. It *must* be easily accessible.

4. *Consistent air humidity is very important. Air that is heavy in humidity does not allow metal and stock oil to dry properly.* Air that is too dry or that is subject to air conditioning can likewise impede proper drying. If your gun room is too dry, install a humidifier. If the room tends to be damp, install a dehumidifier.

5. *Your gun room should have a sink with running water (preferably hot and cold).* The sink must have proper drainage that in no way can back up into the household bathroom, kitchen sink, dishwasher or laundry pipes. A kitchen or bathroom sink is *never* an acceptable place to wash your tools, rubber gloves, implements, or dispose of harmful solutions or waste.

6. *Good lighting is essential.* You'll need fluorescent *and* incandescent lighting. An overhead fluorescent light is best for general lighting. For close-up work, incandescent light is best. An inexpensive goose-neck or swivel lamp that adjusts low to light tight places does a good job. Bolt the light to your workbench so it does not fall over. Make certain the wiring in the room is grounded, safe, and secure,

and that extension cords and other wiring are out of harm's way.

7. *Your workbench must be sturdy and provide a large enough work surface to support your gun, cleaning supplies and equipment.* If the surface is too restricted, the gun will be in danger of teetering off and crashing to the ground, or cans of solvents and other supplies can spill over. A table is not an effective workbench. It is too low and you will have to bend over for close-up work. You can buy a ready-made workbench at most hardware stores or building centers. Or, make your own. Building a workbench can be satisfying, cost effective, and made to suit your space and needs. I provide instructions on page 165.

A gun vise or "cradle" is not a necessity, but it frees up your hands and allows you to work on your gun with greater ease. It also prevents your gun from falling off the workbench and crashing onto the floor.

8. *A gun vise is very helpful.* It is not a necessity, but having one will free your hands to work on your gun and at the same time keep your gun firmly in place and safe from falling. There are several types of vises—a bench vise, barrel vise, checkering vise—each designed for certain uses. The vise you want is called a *gun cradle.* The best is made from oak or oak veneer with a hardwood clamp mechanism with leather pads that support the gun securely while protecting the stock and metal. Rubber feet keep the gun cradle from slipping, or you can drill and bolt it directly onto your workbench, providing you have ample work and storage surface remaining.

9. *Your gun room floor should be easy to sweep and keep clean.* Wall-to-wall carpeting will absorb spills,

grit and grime. Ceramic tile or slate can be slippery when wet. Cement is the least desirable flooring. It is hard and, in cold weather, uncomfortably cold. If you drop your gun on a cement floor, the impact can seriously damage the gun. If you spill solvents on cement, the floor will stain. However, if you have no alternative but a cement floor, a thick rubber floor pad under your entire work area will alleviate some of these problems. A urethane-finished wood or commercial vinyl floor is probably your best bet.

10. *A gun rack is practical and useful if you own more than one gun.* Again, you can make a gun rack that can be built into your workbench, as shown on page 164, or a self-standing floor rack. Either way, be sure the rack is bolted securely to the floor or

A fireproof, burglarproof (and childproof!) gun vault is the only practical and safe way to store your guns. Be sure to install desiccant packs or a Golden Rod to keep another culprit at bay—rust-loving moisture.

workbench, otherwise the weight of the gun will cause it to fall over.

11. *A gun vault is the only practical way for you to safely store your guns, keep them away from children, and protect them from fire and theft.* Gun vaults come in a wide range of sizes, styles and costs—you can get the lockable steel variety at most discount superstores for under $100, but these are neither fireproof or very secure. You can spend thousands of dollars on a state-of-the-art, custom glass and climate-controlled safe complete with burglar alarm, if you have enough guns—and means—to warrant one. Your best bet is to get an inflammable, solid steel gun vault from Winchester, Browning, Remington, Fort Knox or National Security Safe Company, among others.

Chapter Three

CLEANING TOOLS & SUPPLIES

I. SHOTGUN CLEANING-RODS

THERE ARE SEVERAL FACTORS involved in the cleaning-rod you use in your shotgun. It must be smaller in diameter than the bore. If it is too tight, you run the risk of jamming a patch or cleaning head, or the rod itself can lodge and become an obstruction. Never use force on *any* part of a gun. If a rod is too large, or is thrust into the bore, you can damage the forcing cone or choke, or create longitudinal scratches that can only be removed by lapping, a gunsmith procedure. Conversely, a cleaning-rod or cleaning-rod head that is too small will make inadequate contact, leaving residue in the bore and defeating the purpose of cleaning.

Cleaning-rods are designed for standard bores from 10- to 28-gauge and .410-caliber, and are available anywhere gun supplies are sold. If you shoot a rare or antiquated gun, such as an 8-gauge or 24-bore, a jointed aluminum rod with patches will serve; however, consult with your gunsmith to see if a custom brass or wooden rod can be made. *Never* use a rifle or pistol cleaning-rod in a shotgun. These are meant for smaller, rifled bores.

Though all cleaning-rods serve the same purpose, each type has different attributes—and drawbacks. For example, a jointed aluminum rod is fine for occasional field use but less than ideal at the workbench. Any one-piece rod is an awkward traveling accessory. A pull-through is portable, convenient and effectively removes fouling, but cannot dislodge an obstruction.

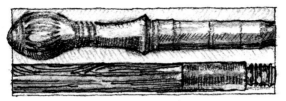

ENGLISH-STYLE WOODEN CLEANING-ROD

A fine complement for a double gun is an English-style wooden cleaning-rod that is fitted with brass ferrules to couple two- and three-piece types. With normal use, wood or brass cannot scratch or abrade a bore. Wooden cleaning-rods come in shotgun accessory kits or can be bought separately. Most are turned from straight-grain hardwoods such as mahogany, teak, birch, maple and hickory, which are very strong. The length of a wooden rod runs 32 to 39 inches, depending on the gauge and make. The cost is about $20 with cleaning heads extra. The finest rod I know of is ebony with gold-plated brass ferrules from Galazan. It will put you back about $75.

The disadvantage of a wooden cleaning-rod is that no matter how strong the variety, wood is breakable. Ferrules can pull apart from the shaft if the glue gives way. If a cleaning head is seated incorrectly, the female threads in the rod tip can be stripped. If a wooden rod is used with force to pound out a bore obstruction and breaks or expands, then the rod itself can become an obstruction. Removal then becomes a professional gunsmith procedure. In an extreme case, a rod can get so tightly impacted that it becomes impossible to dislodge—making the barrel need to be replaced. Depending on the gun, replacing a barrel is one of the most expensive and critical operations in the art and craft of gunmaking. If this happens to a fine double gun, the cost can be prohibitive. It is not unheard of to pay $15,000 *and up* for replacement barrels for a London Best.

Given care and conscientious handling, a wooden cleaning-rod should last the lifetime of your gun. Care for it like a gunstock, with periodic oiling. Polish the brass, otherwise it will turn black (though this will not harm a bore.)

NOTE: USA-made rods have American standard threads that *do not* accept English threaded cleaning heads—or vice versa.

AND A WORD OF CAUTION: A .410-caliber barrel is so small in diameter that a 33-inch rod designed to fit that bore can break easily. It would be safer to run a cleaning patch through the bore using a brass rod designed to fit a .410.

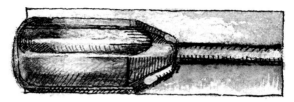

NYLON-COATED ALUMINUM CLEANING-ROD

Nylon-coated or anodized aluminum cleaning-rods are available in one- or two-pieces types, in 10- to 28-gauge and are a good solution for .410 caliber. The tough coating prevents bore abrasion. Those made of aircraft aluminum are durable, lightweight and cost about $25. This is a good foul weather field rod because it won't break or swell like a wooden rod and can handle most obstructions. It comes with a patch loop and adapter for cleaning heads that are sold separately. This rod only needs a light wiping to stay clean. Not pretty, but it's useful and does a great job.

BRASS CLEANING-ROD

A brass cleaning rod is heavy, durable, and will not abrade or damage a gun bore. With care, one will last your lifetime. The tip is threaded for a patch loop and will accept cleaning heads that you buy separately. Prices run the gamut. I have seen some as reasonable as $25, and others that are several times more. This is an ideal cleaning-rod for the workbench, but it is awkward and cumbersome for field use and not something you would necessarily want to lug along on your travels. Brass is easy to wipe clean of solvents and oil, and a little polish will keep it bright.

ONE-PASS "WOOL" MOP

This lightweight, three-piece plastic shaft cleaning-rod is wrapped with "wool" (synthetic fleece) and swabs a bore in one pass—hence, its name. Get a couple—one for use with solvent, another for oiling the bore. The American standard thread tip accepts phosphor bronze brushes and other cleaning heads. I've only seen these in 12-gauge. *Do not attempt to force it through smaller bores!* It can be washed in hot, soapy water, but the fleece eventually loses its resilience. Nonetheless, this inexpensive yet effective bench or travel rod can be readily replaced whenever one wears out.

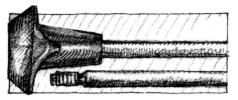

JOINTED ALUMINUM CLEANING-ROD

Available at virtually every hardware store, this sort of rod is inexpensive, serviceable, and good for travel or field use, but I do not recommend it as your sole bench rod for one very real reason: An aluminum rod can cause bore wear. Aluminum is a soft metal, but when it is exposed to air, a thin coating of *aluminum oxide* develops. Aluminum oxide, the principle component of sandpaper, is one of the hardest substances known to man. Certainly, pack an aluminum rod and some patches, solvent and oil in your gear bag. However, use it carefully and only occasionally.

PULL-THROUGH

A pull-through is a handy cleaning device that you can stuff into your shooting coat pocket and take out whenever you need to swipe the bore of powder fouling, saltwater, etc. There are two types. One is a pliant, washable bore mop swaddled in a nylon cord. The other is a braided steel cord with a tip adapter that accepts cleaning heads. Nothing beats a pull-through for on-the-spot cleaning. However, it is no substitute for a workbench rod. This has been a standard military field-cleaning device since breechloaders came into use in the 1880s. It will *not* dislodge obstructions.

This unique cleaning set by Orvis features a braided pull-through with screw-in cleaning heads that stuffs into your shooting coat pocket for quick bore cleaning on the field or at the range.

There are various types of cleaning heads and each has a different application. Sometimes they are called English brush heads, or simply bristle brushes. There is no outward difference between those made in Britain and the United States—but beware. English-made brushes screw into rods with British threads, while USA-made rods and heads have American standard threads. Rods and heads with American standard threads are not interchangeable with British threads.

II. BORE CLEANING HEADS

THERE IS QUITE A VARIETY of bore cleaning heads and each is designed to serve a particular purpose. All cleaning-rods, with the exception of a nylon pull-through, are made for use with screw-in cleaning heads. Purchase yours when you buy your cleaning-rod so you're sure they fit. Not all cleaning heads fit all cleaning-rods. British-threaded heads and rods do not interchange with rods and cleaning heads with American standard threads. Rods and cleaning heads made in England are available in the U.S. only through gun shops and gun supply catalogues that specialize in fine imported guns. American made rods and cleaning heads are available pretty much anywhere that sporting goods are sold and through most hunting and gun parts catalogues.

PHOSPHOR BRONZE BRUSH
Made for English or American standard threads

This brush is used to scrub the bore of heavy powder fouling, plastic residue, and caked or hardened grime. The bristles are made of phosphor bronze, a metal that is softer than barrel steel, or a DuPont nylon called Tynex™, and looped or wound around a brass or stainless steel shank. A safety loop tip prevents damage to the breech faces. You will need one of these for tough jobs. It costs about $6. Best results always come when you use the right brush with the right solvent made for the type of fouling in the bore.

Here's a valuable suggestion from a friend who is a lifelong shooter and top authority on guns and ammunition. After a day of sporting clays or driven birds, when you've put a lot of rounds through your gun and plastic residue has really built up, swipe the bore of your gun with a phosphor bronze brush dipped in a powerful solvent. Leave the bore wet for a couple of hours, then swab it thoroughly. You will be amazed how much residue is removed by this method. After the bore is thoroughly clean, apply a thin coat of oil with a cotton bore mop or patch. It is extremely important that you oil the bore before putting the gun away. Solvents, especially the modern, more powerful ones, evaporate and leave a bore bone-dry. Without a thin coat of oil, your bore will invite rust, which creates pitting.

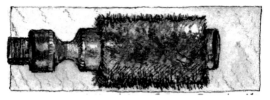

BOAR BRISTLE BRUSH
Made for English or American standard threads

This brush is less aggressive than a phosphor bronze brush and is used to clean the bore of dust and fouling after light shooting. The best are made with real boar hair; less expensive ones have synthetic bristles. This brush is not appropriate for oiling, as it will streak the bore and leave excess. Use with solvent and a light scrub motion. Run a cotton patch through the bore, and another, then another until the last patch comes out slightly gray, thereby indicating that all traces of fouling and grime are gone from all surfaces of the bore. Apply a few drops of oil to a cotton bore mop or gun patch and give the bore a final swab.

In rifled guns, phosphor bronze and boar bristle brushes should be inserted from the breech, not the muzzle of the gun, in order to protect the grooves at the muzzle. The same applies to a shotgun. You can "bell" the choke so that it tapers outward at the muzzle and throws off the patterning. This is the kind of damage you want to avoid. You have no choice but to run a rod through the muzzle of a gun if the barrel does not take down. Use a jointed aluminum rod with a patch and a lot of care. Always run the brush *completely* through the bore before pulling it back through the barrel. If you try to remove a bore brush inside the barrel, you can twist or break the bristles. (Not the case with Tynex™ brushes.)

TORNADO BRUSH
Made for English or American standard threads

This is the most aggressive commercial brush available and should only be used for heavy fouling—and *always* with lubricant and a light touch. On one hand, a tornado brush can burnish a bore and give it a brilliant finish. It effectively removes stubborn plastic fouling caused by shot protectors. However, when used dry, a tornado brush can seriously scratch or damage a bore. *Never* scrub or use vigorous action with this cleaning head. Remember, a bore that has been scratched will need to be polished or lapped by a gunsmith.

COTTON BORE MOP
Made for English or American standard threads

A cotton bore mop can be used with solvent for light cleaning, but its primary use is to swab the entire bore with an even coat of oil. This cleaning head is made of dense cotton tufts twisted around a stainless steel or brass shank. It uniformly contacts all surfaces of the bore (providing the mop corresponds with the gun gauge.) *Never* force a mop that is too large into the bore! If you try, it may get stuck. A mop that has been used with oil can be kept clean by washing it in hot water with a little detergent. Ring it, then prop it up to air dry.

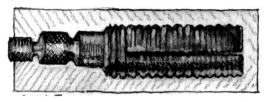

BRITISH BRASS SPLIT JAG
For use only with tow. Made for English threads only.

A jag is the British equivalent of a cotton bore mop. It is used with tow, which is a wad of loose cotton threads. The jag is attached to the cleaning-rod. A wad of tow is pulled off the bundle, stuffed into the slot in the jag, wound around the head, lubricated, then pushed through the bore. You can apply solvent or oil to tow. Tow is thrown away after use. Although a split jag looks like it ought to be used with cleaning patches, it can not. Just try, and you will surely jam a patch in the bore.

III. GUN CLEANING ACCESSORIES

THERE ARE ALL SORTS of cleaning accessories, but not all are appropriate for shotgun use. Those made for rifles, handguns and blackpowder guns are meant to clean the groves in rifling and should never be used in smoothbores. Shotguns are smoothbores. (Unless it is a *rifled shotgun*, which is intended for use with slugs. Rifles are illegal for hunting whitetail in certain deer wildlife management units in some states.)

There are, however, tools that are not part of a standard gun-cleaning kit that are useful and can facilitate certain cleaning jobs. Some are appropriate to certain types of shotguns, and some to specific makes. All are relatively inexpensive and generally available in sporting goods stores and gun supply catalogues.

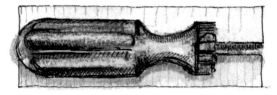

PIN PUSHER

A pin pusher is *not* a universal tool. It is used to remove the pins that hold the trigger group on Remington pumps and semi-automatics. Removal of the trigger group by the operator facilitates cleaning in certain guns, but this is the exception, not the rule for models such as the Remington Models 870, 1100, 48 and 1187. Otherwise, *never* try to disassemble the trigger group of *any* shotgun. This is strictly a gunsmith procedure. Assume that any tools that come with your gun are meant for use by a gunsmith—*not you*. Do so, and you will end up with a handful of parts.

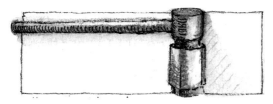

CHOKE TUBE WRENCH

A choke tube wrench is a tool that is usually
provided with all guns that have been fitted with
screw-in choke tubes. It is designed to remove the
tubes without damaging the tube, choke or muzzle.
Some tubes are designed to be put in with the
fingers and should be finger-tightened only, thus
eliminating the need for a choke tube wrench.
Never use pliers or any other tool on finger-
tightened tubes. Choke tubes should be removed
regularly and cleaned as you would a gun. This
prevents them from becoming rusted or fouled in
place, which is a serious problem.

Should this happen, there is a device called a STUCK CHOKE TUBE REMOVAL TOOL. This is a gunsmith tool and is *not* recommended for use by the shooter. It is designed to remove a choke tube that has stuck in the muzzle because of fouling, rust, damaged threads or other common problems. It will not remove a choke that is bulged. Improperly used, you can kink or otherwise seriously damage the threaded portion of the choke tube or the muzzle of the gun—and create for yourself a bigger problem than you had to start with.

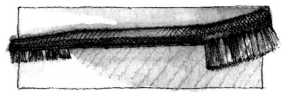

UTILITY BRUSH

This useful cleaning tool removes accumulated grease and hardened oil from the extractors, triggers, top lever and hammers, and can knock out plastic fouling in ported barrels or choke tubes. The best kind has phosphor bronze bristles, which can be used on any metal surface without damage *providing it is used with suitable solvents*. Always use a gentle scrubbing motion with *any* brush and always with a solvent. Any brush can scratch metal and damage blueing, case colors, stock finish and even engraving if it is used vigorously or without a solvent or lubricant.

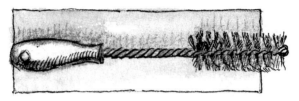

CHAMBER BRUSH

A chamber brush is a useful tool for the shooter who puts so many rounds through a gun that an egg could fry on the barrel. When a gun is used to that extent—whether on the sporting clays range or shooting driven birds—you're going to accumulate serious plastic fouling in the chamber and in the bores. A phosphor bronze chamber brush used with a strong solvent like Hoppe's Castrol GunStripper™ will loosen tough deposits. Afterwards, wipe the gunmetal thoroughly with a clean, dry, soft cloth, then lubricate the parts lightly with oil.

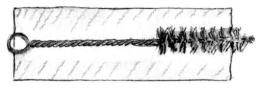

SHOTGUN PORT BRUSH

If your gun has ported barrels or ported choke tubes, a shotgun port brush will knock out wad residue and carbon fouling. This thin, stainless steel brush is designed specifically to fit the ports and *must* be used with cleaning solvent.

STEEL WOOL

Steel wool in #000 or #0000 grit is desirable for removing light rust from metal parts. Although fine grits are the least abrasive, *any* steel wool, if used dry and with rigorous action, can scratch metal. *Always* use steel wool with a solvent or lubricant. For our purposes, *do not* use steel wool on your stock, as you can dull or distort the finish.

Oiling or wiping down your gunstock is as important as lubricating the metal parts of your gun. It is an intrinsic part of gun maintenance, without which the gun cleaning process is incomplete.

CLEANING PATCHES & GUN RAGS

Do not underestimate the importance of working with the right stuff. Cleaning patches are available in synthetic fabrics, but the *only* type of patch I recommend are those made from pure cotton. Cotton is more absorbent and simply does a better job. As for gun rags, do not reach for anything in your household rag bin. Tightly woven cotton or light flannel is what you need. Denim is too coarse for most applications and like synthetics, does not absorb well. If you do not have any rags handy, tear up an old white cotton sheet (make sure it is 100-percent cotton, not polycotton). Do this and you'll be in rags for a long time. Remember, rags are washable, but because they are exposed to solvents, *never* put them in the washing machine or dryer. Wash separately by hand and line-dry.

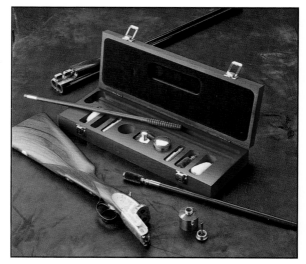

Made in England, this handsome deluxe gun accessory kit features rosewood and gold-plated accessories. Nothing beats a set like this for British-made guns—however, it is only appropriate for cleaning-rods and accessories with British threads, and the jag only works with tow. Screwdrivers in this kit are made to fit British and continental screwheads. They will not be satisfactory on the screws used in American-made guns.

IV. DELUXE ACCOUTERMENTS

INSTEAD OF BUYING INDIVIDUAL gun cleaning tools and accessories, you may wish to invest in a gun cleaning kit. Most include a cleaning-rod and patch loop, bore cleaning head, bore cleaner, oil and patches. Deluxe kits include additional accessories or accouterments, such as extra cleaning heads, while the top-of-the-line variety include snap caps, choke gauges, *turnscrews* (gun screwdrivers made for British guns), oil bottles, grease jars, firing pin canisters and chamber gauges. Just keep in mind that he who has the most toys . . . has paid for more toys. What you choose should depend upon what you need specifically for the gun you shoot. For example, a deluxe English accessory kit is pretty highfalutin for use with a Browning A-5. Not only would turnscrews and other Best gun accessories be entirely useless on an A-5, but the idea of owning a deluxe accessory kit that costs more than your gun doesn't make a whole lot of sense either. Conversely, if you do own a fine British, Italian or continental gun, it would behoove you to have such a cleaning set, which is designed specifically to complement a high-grade double gun.

Some gun cleaning kits are sold by gauge, and others contain cleaning heads for several gauges that screw into a universal adapter. The kit you decide upon should be in keeping with the gauge and type of guns you own. I cannot stress enough the importance of using cleaning heads that correspond with the gauge of your gun. Anything else will either be ineffective or troublesome.

UNIVERSAL CHAMBER LENGTH GAUGE

A chamber gauge is a useful tool that measures the length of the chamber of a shotgun. Embossed, brass "fingers" in bore sizes from .410 caliber to 10-gauge measure the chamber length in inches. This will tell you the correct length of shell you should be firing in your gun. Granted, you should know your gun well enough to say whether it shoots a standard American 2¾-inch shell or a British 2½ cartridge. However, if you are contemplating the purchase of a previously owned or vintage gun, you must first ascertain the chamber length. Two-inch, 2½-inch and 2⁹/₁₆-inch shotgun shells are uncommon and generally only available from specialty dealers.

Remember, you can always fire a shorter shell in a longer chamber, but the reverse is untrue. *Never attempt to fire a shell that is too long for the chamber.* A long shell in a short chamber will vastly increase the pressure in the forcing cone, resulting in a gun that you can't open because it is swollen shut from pressure. In an extreme case, you can bulge or split the barrel. No matter what the length of the chamber, never shoot a nitro load in a blackpowder gun that is not proofed for modern loads.

GREASE JAR

A grease (or Vaseline) jar can hold your favorite gun grease, such as Rig™, Gunslick™, Tetra Gun G™, or Brownell's Action Lube Plus™. Perhaps the small size of the jar should be a reminder to use grease sparingly. Apply grease with a light touch and you will avoid the need for your gun to be stripped and professionally cleaned of hardened grease buildup later. Use a cotton swab or your fingertip. Wipe away excess afterwards with a clean, *dry* cotton cloth.

"Classic" Plated Oil Jars

There are round oil jars and there are square oil jars. Put oil in one and solvent in the other and don't confuse them. Attached to the underside of the screw top is a flat wand applicator that holds ¹⁄₁₀ ml. of oil or solvent that can reach deeply and directly into the working parts of the action. That's plenty for most purposes. Use a soft rag to wipe away any excess. Remember, *clean thoroughly and oil sparingly*. A dip of this applicator will keep you from oiling with a heavy hand.

FIRING PIN CANISTER *(for hammer guns)*

Usually turned from ebony, a firing pin canister theoretically holds firing pins. However, its place in deluxe cleaning kits is a bit of a throw-back to past times when firing pins were (and still are, in high-grade guns) a handmade proposition, so extra pins were generally kept on hand should one break during shooting season. If so, the shooting gentleman's gunsmith would have one at the ready for a relatively speedy emergency repair. The replacement of a firing pin in any gun, let alone a double gun, is a gunsmith operation, as we discussed on page 7. Most over/under shotguns do have separate firing pins, but they are extremely difficult to get at and, in order to do so, require complete disassembly of the gun—not an amateur operation. The firing pin of a side-by-side is on the nose of the hammer (as a rule). In the event of damage, that means an *extensive, costly professional* repair of the pin or possibly replacement of the hammer. This is the case in American side-by-sides, such as those made by Fox, Parker, the Winchester Model 21, and British and continental guns. If you happen to have extra firing pins, regard them as something you can take to your gunsmith for him to put in.

NOTE: Firing pins for autoloaders and pump guns are about 3½-inches long and won't fit into a firing pin canister.

BASIC GUN CLEANING PROCEDURE

Step One

Make sure the gun is empty. If it is a double, break the action and make sure both barrels are empty. If it is a pump or semi-automatic, open the action and make sure the chamber is empty. Turn over and make sure the magazine is clear.

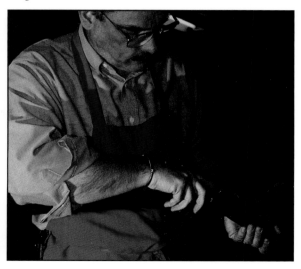

Step Two

Moisten a phosphor bronze bristle brush with powder solvent. Pass it back and forth through the bore five to ten times, as needed, from the breech to the muzzle. Be sure the brush goes all the way through the bore before pulling it back.

Step Three

Attach slotted rod tip to the cleaning rod and put in a clean, dry cotton patch of the correct size. Pass through the bore several times. Repeat twice more with a fresh patch each time or until patch is a gray color. Patch will be a gray color, not white, and must be free of black residue.

Using a bore light or strong light source, inspect the bore carefully. If fouling still appears, proceed to more aggressive cleaning. For severe fouling, especially plastic residue, wet patch with bore cleaner and run it through the bore several times until well coated. If the barrel is hanging on the gun, keep the barrel pointing down to avoid having loosened fouling run back into the action or other moving parts. Wait five minutes. Then, using a phosphor bronze bristle brush, scrub bore ten times, pushing the brush all the way through the bore from the breech to the muzzle. Next, clean out bore with dry patches until all trace of residue is gone and the patch comes out gray.

NOTE: For stubborn plastic fouling, coat the bore with bore cleaner and let the barrel rest for an hour or two before following the process above.

Step Four

Apply degreaser to a patch or spray directly down the bore. Be careful not to contact wood or plastic stocks. Wipe out quickly with dry patches. Allow to dry—this will happen within seconds.

Step Five

Again, inspect bore. If fouling *still* appears, apply bore cleaner to a tornado brush and gently run through the bore five times. Use degreaser as before. *Do not use dry!* Repeat until bore is spotless.

Step Six

Immediately oil cleaning patch with rust preventative and run through the bore several times, leaving a thin, even film. Then, apply a gun oil to all metal parts that have come in contact with degreaser. Work the action several times to allow oil to get deep into the working parts.

Final Step

Wipe oil-finished stocks with oil, lacquer-finished stocks with wax, or synthetic or epoxy-finished stocks with water. Wipe fingerprints off gunmetal with a damp (not wet) cloth, then a final rub with a silicone cloth or a rag moistened with gun oil. Lock your gun away in a gun vault or closet.

End of the season for pumps and autos

Remove trigger group. Spray with degreaser, using plastic nozzle extension to get into every crack and crevice. Do the same for interior of action, pointing down to prevent getting it on the stock. Do the same for all interior parts, such as the bolt, shell stop, etc. When dirt and fouling have been flushed away, wipe with soft cloth and allow to dry. Then apply a thin film of rust preventative oil to all metal parts.

Oil, wax or wipe down stocks as appropriate.

End of the season for double guns

Use nitro solvent or bore cleaner to clean out extractors, forearm latch, underlugs, contact points of breech— anywhere that shows fouling. Use degreaser if necessary to obtain clean surface, but do not use spray degreaser on the action. This will remove protection from interior working parts. Apply a thin film of rust preventative oil to all metal parts.

Oil, wax or wipe down stocks as appropriate.

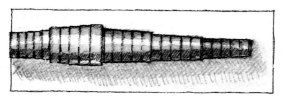

CHOKE GAUGE

A choke gauge is used to determine the choke of a gun. It is placed in the bore at the muzzle. A choke gauge is marked incrementally from cylinder to full, and 12-gauge to .410-caliber. This is a useful tool to keep on hand if you go to gun shows or gun shops regularly to hunt for previously owned guns. On some deluxe English cleaning rods, a choke gauge is incorporated into the handle of the rod, which then unscrews to reveal a turnscrew in the fluted wood handle, such as Galazan's, shown on page 72.

Working with solvents can be dangerous. Take your time and use your head.

Chapter Four
WORKING WITH SOLVENTS & LUBRICANTS

SPERM OIL, PARAFFIN OIL, LARD OIL AND CARBON tetrachloride have long been replaced by modern, technologically refined solvents and lubricants formulated to insure a gun's optimum performance and function under diverse and severe weather and firing conditions. All solvents made specifically for cleaning gunmetal are effective and will work, if used properly. A blast of degreaser will remove accumulated powder fouling, oil and hardened crud, dust and other sludge that lodges in tight places—and it will also remove valuable lubrication that will have to be replaced. Working with solvents can be dangerous. Just take your time and use your head. That means taking precautions *before* you begin cleaning your gun.

Every time a cartridge is fired, a shotgun bore is exposed to fouling from powder, plastic and metal that can accumulate and form deposits that affect a gun's function and, in extreme cases, reliability. A gun must be able to perform in any situation and condition in the field or on the range, and be in ready condition to encounter hostile elements, such as driving wind and rain, mud, snow and saltwater. A gun should work just as dependably in sub-zero cold as in sweltering heat, and there are solvents to insure a gun can work in such extremes. A well-maintained gun can make the difference between a clean kill and a crippled bird, or get you that crucial point in a sporting clays tournament. The right solvents and lubricant are

insurance for maintaining the optimum performance of your gun.

There are two types of solvents: strong solvents
and stronger solvents. All solvents are hazardous—
to breathe, ingest, or contact your eyes or skin—
any contact on your person. Do not let the fine
print on the can suggest otherwise. For example,
there is one product on the market that clearly
states on its label, "Product is not poisonous;
however may be fatal or harmful if swallowed."
This is sort of like suggesting that guns aren't
dangerous unless you get in the way of a bullet.
Work slowly and carefully whenever you handle
solvents of any kind. Assume that any solvent you
use is not going to be good for you. For your safety,
never clean a gun without the following products.

Safety Glasses

Wearing safety glasses can save your sight. *All* gun solvents are eye irritants. The manufacturers' labels will tell you to wash your eye thoroughly with tepid water and call a doctor if you get their product in your eye. The operative word here is *doctor*. That means you may need immediate medical attention. Solvents are caustic and irritating, can cause severe pain, and most certainly have the potential to do permanent damage. It is not hard to get solvent in your eye if you are working with an aerosol or spray, or if you drop a can of solvent and some of the contents splashes. I cannot stress enough how imperative it is that you wear safety glasses. In fact, it is a good precaution to wear safety glasses in the gun room at all times, just as you would on the field or at the range. Commercial safety glasses are made of clear plastic, usually with vented side panels, and will fit over your regular glasses if you wear corrective lenses. If you are a contact lens wearer and get solvent in your eye, you must remove the contact immediately and throw it away. It is now contaminated. There is nothing you can do to insure the contact will be free of solvent, even after a thorough cleaning.

PROPER VENTILATION

FRESH AIR CIRCULATION IS CRUCIAL. Any work area where you use solvents should either be exposed to open air or have an adequate exhaust fan to prevent concentration of fumes. Toxic fumes in a closed space displace the oxygen in the air, build up, and become extremely hazardous. Fumes can burn your lungs and can even be life threatening. Take preventative measures. For example, do not assume that opening a window a few inches is enough. Whenever you use solvent, there must be an obvious flow of fresh air in the room at all times. A fan with no direct outside vent is inadequate. Don't attempt to ventilate a 12 x 12-foot room with an eight-inch fan. You can't.

Rubber Gloves

JUST AS A SOLVENT WILL REMOVE oil from gun parts, it will also remove oil from your skin, leaving it dry and cracked. Some solvents can penetrate the skin, causing irritation or worse. Some of the stronger solvents can destroy the epidermal layer and will cause the skin to die and slough off. If solvent gets on your skin and you cannot wash away the burning sensation, seek medical attention.

If you get solvent on your skin, immediately use hot, soapy water and wash the affected area completely *at least twice*, making sure you rinse thoroughly between washings.

You can avoid skin irritation or burns caused by solvents by wearing a pair of good rubber gloves, which are available at most hardware stores. They should fit well. If the gloves are too tight, they will restrict movement. If they are too loose, you will not be able to hold cans and cleaning tools properly. Some solvents can disintegrate rubber, in which case the fingertips of the gloves become soft and sticky. My solution to this problem is to buy disposable neoprene gloves, which are sold in most hardware stores. They are inexpensive (sold individually or in boxes of 100), will keep solvent from getting on your hands, and yet are thin enough to make handling small parts easy. Once you are finished using them, toss them in the garbage. Do not save them for another day. NOTE: Always make sure the garbage is not near a heat source, as anything that has come in contact with solvent—whether it's neoprene or rubber gloves, paper towels, gun rags or steel wool—is potentially combustible.

Shop Apron

WEAR WORK CLOTHES in your gun room to avoid soiling or damaging your good clothes. Always wear a shop apron. This not only protects whatever you are wearing, but if solvent splashes on you, it will not seep into your clothes. The best is a leather shop apron, which is available through Brownells.

KNOW YOUR SOLVENTS

SOLVENTS ARE MADE TO DO A JOB. Almost any solvent on the market today designed for cleaning guns will do the job and do it well. This is because improvements in solvents for cleaning guns stem from developments in industrial and high tech applications. However, it is up to you to know the qualities of each solvent and lubricant. This is particularly important because of their toxic, flammable and dangerous qualities. *Know their uses and the limits of their applications.* The following are a few tips about solvents.

ACETONE is exceedingly flammable. A lit cigarette around an acetone-based product makes an *instant* flame-thrower.

Petroleum Distillates are also highly flammable. Be *sure* to use eye and hand protection, and have proper ventilation before using a product with a petroleum distillate base.

Read the Caution statements for each product carefully. For example, do not induce vomiting if petroleum distillates are swallowed. Even products that purport to not irritate eyes or skin can make this warning. The fact is, petroleum distillates *do* burn skin. Vomiting will only induce further damage to the mouth, throat, stomach and esophagus.

Just because a product claims it is not damaging to the ozone layer does not mean it is not damaging to you. Inhaling a spray or aerosol solvent in a restricted place or close-up when you are outdoors can cause dizziness, disorientation or other nervous system reactions.

All "super cleaners" are designed to evaporate completely and almost instantly, leaving the metal chemically clean but bone-dry and thereby vulnerable to moisture and other rusting agents. You must lubricate metal with a good-quality oil or metal preservative *immediately* after using a degreaser or other gun cleaning solvent.

Most bore cleaning solvents can dissolve oil and varnish gunstock finishes. Since these are also meant to dissolve plastic residue, keep them away from plastic stocks as well. Remove the barrel or gunmetal part you are cleaning so it is separate from the stock. If this is not possible, spray the solvent directly on a patch, bore mop, or cleaning head and work carefully and slowly so the solvent does not to come in contact with the stock. Do not over-saturate the patch or cleaning head. If you do, you are apt to puddle the solvent (which is now a liquid), which can seep between the areas of wood-to-metal fit.

Aerosol sprays work best between 72- and 100-degrees Fahrenheit. Do not spray an aerosol near electrical outlets or any source of ignition, such as pilot lights, space heaters, camp stoves or cigarette lighters. A lit match or cigarette can turn into a torch. Remember, *aerosol is compressed gas.* Do not puncture, incinerate, or store an aerosol can in temperatures over 120-degrees. Also, keep aerosol cans out of direct sunlight.

A fired projectile creates high bore temperatures that bake mineral or wax-based compounds into a viscous substance. This substance bonds with plastic residue and fouling, which is why it is so important to make sure the bore is thoroughly cleaned and lightly oiled. If not, firing problems can occur that invariably will worsen in cold weather as the crud solidifies.

Use only the solvents you need to do the job!
Over-cleaning can damage a gun!

TYPES OF SOLVENTS

POWDER SOLVENT—*the first step*

Powder solvent removes the nitro residue that comes from firing. This is the first solvent you should reach for after you come in from the field or range. It is used mainly in the bore but should be applied to all working parts of the gun that come in contact with powder fouling, such as the bolts, trigger group, operating handle, magazine tube, barrel ports and choke tubes. In most cases, powder solvent is enough to do the job after normal firing. There are many brands to choose from, including the classic, Hoppes No. 9™, and the military's choice, Break Free Powder Blast™. Powder solvent does not remove plastic residue. For that you'll need something stronger to cut through the crud . . .

BORE CLEANER—*only for heavy fouling*

. . . And that's bore cleaner. This powerful solvent is formulated to soften hardened residue and is far more aggressive than powder solvent. You can spray the aerosol variety directly into the bore, but I favor direct application with a well-moistened gun patch instead. If you spray the aerosol, excess solvent can run down the barrel, into the working parts, and over the stock. Bore cleaner will remove lubrication from extractors or ejectors, springs, inside the magazine tube—any gunmetal it contacts—so you *must* relubricate afterwards. Use Iosso®, Birchwood Casey Super Strength Bore Scrubber™, Jim Brobst Non-embedding Compound®, Brownell's Shotgun Wad Solvent® or one of the others sparingly and *only* if residue remains *after* using powder solvent.

DEGREASER—*essential prior to oiling*

Now that you've dissolved and loosened powder fouling and plastic residue from the bore and working parts, you have to remove lingering residue with degreaser. Degreasers such as Gun Sav'R™ Kwik-Flush, Brownell's™ TCE, or LPS® ZeroTri, will instantly evaporate, leaving gunmetal chemically clean. Apply to the barrel, receiver, chamber, gas ports, choke tubes—anywhere grime accumulates. Again, I prefer to keep control over the cleaning area by using brushes and gun patches instead of aerosol. Degreaser can also remove oil and lacquer stock finish and damage plastic! If you want to use an aerosol to flush out the bore, remove the barrels and spray into the chamber, keeping the muzzle down and away from you. Don't flood the bore!

Rust Preventative—*highly advisable*

After using a degreaser, your bore is chemically clean but it is also vulnerable to corrosion and rust. Immediately replace gun oil and lubricants so your gun will work smoothly and efficiently. Among many are Birchwood Casey Sheath® Rust Preventative and Brownell's™ Aerosol Rust Preventative No. 2, which penetrate and lubricate the metal parts of the gun while lifting out and displacing any remaining moisture from metal pores and crevices. Nothing looks smoother than a bright bore, yet metallurgical studies show that polished gunmetal resembles the Himalayas rather than glass. Never assume your gun is completely free of moisture. You may think it is, but chances are it is not.

Note: *Anything that can dissolve rust can dissolve blueing. Be careful!*

OIL AND LUBRICATION—*absolutely essential*

Applying oil and lubricants is the essential final step in the gun cleaning procedure. Many products do the job, but first you need to know what job your gun needs to do. For example, Nyoil, Hoppes™ No. 9 Lubricating Oil, Gunslick™, Shooter's Choice™ All-Weather High-Tech grease, Brownell's Action Lube Plus™, and Break Free CLP™ (which is safe on wood, plastic and metal) are excellent for use at the bench. For quick work in the field, use Castrol/Hoppes No. 9 FieldCleaner™. These keep the gun working smoothly in temperatures to -50 degrees F. For high performance, a metallic sulfide based lubricant, such as Gun Sav'R™, is best for a competition gun that has hundreds of rounds fired through it on any given day.

Other Gun Care Products

There are other gun care products on the market that you may wish to incorporate into your personal cleaning ritual. One, for example, is gun wax, a longtime means of keeping gunmetal and oil-finished or varnished gunstocks in top condition. Most are made with natural oils, such as Flitz®, which is made with carnauba oil and beeswax. Just remember that wax can cause buildup, so use it sparingly. I discuss this in the next chapter.

There are solvents such as GunSav'r Armor-Kote™ which have been developed for long-term storage protection. This works very much like cosmoline, which is used to pack new (usually military) weapons from rust and corrosion. The thing to remember about products made for longtime storage is that they do not absolve you from checking your gun regularly, nor can you fire your gun until the coating, which tends to be sticky, is completely removed.

Choke lube is used mostly by competition clay or driven bird shooters to lubricate interchangeable chokes. Hoppe's™ Choke Tube Lube or Birchwood Casey® Choke Tube Lube are good lubes. They're specifically formulated to prevent stuck choke tubes, a problem that arises when fast firing produces high temperatures that can cause screw-in chokes to expand. It is also useful during extended storage to prevent choke tubes from freezing in place.

The novice should stay clear of metal polish because used improperly, it can damage blueing. WD-40® is an excellent water-displacing compound, but it is too volatile to prevent rust.

Chapter Five

GUNSTOCKS

WHEN IT COMES TO BUYING a new or previously owned gun, it is the gunstock that generally commands the most attention. A gun is no good for a shooter unless the gun fit is right, and likewise a gun is no pleasure if the aesthetics or qualities of the stock fail to conform to your needs. Whether it is a finely figured Turkish walnut stock, laminate, or synthetic stock, many factors go into choosing the right one for you. However, the care of a gunstock is relatively easy compared to the care of gunmetal. Of course, if you get into stock refinishing—well, that's another book entirely.

Although we've focused on how to care for gunmetal, a gun is not entirely clean unless the stock has been cleaned as well. In most cases, this merely requires wiping the gun down. However, there are considerations and concerns about what you should and should not do.

Here's a good, simple rule: For guns with natural finishes, use natural products. For guns with synthetic finishes, use synthetic products.

OIL-FINISHED STOCKS

FOR GUNS WITH OIL-FINISHED STOCKS, apply a thin coat of stock finishing oil. My favorite is Dem-Bart™ Stock and Checker Oil. Whenever the stock begins to look dry, apply a thin coat with a gun rag, making sure you cover the entire stock uniformly. Leave it on for five minutes, then rub it off thoroughly. The stock should be a little tacky to the touch. Be careful not to allow any to get under the top lever, safety, triggers, etc., because it can literally gum up the works. If this happens, the gun has to be taken apart and professionally cleaned. If the gun appears to need another coat, wait 24-hours before reapplying. Although the stock may appear dry, it is not. If you apply another coat too quickly, it will remove the first coat. Repeat until the stock has a uniform luster. Do not use the gun for a couple of days after the final coat so that it can dry properly. Keep the gun propped up securely on its butt or in a gun vise or cradle so that the wood does not come in contact with any surface. Be sure it is in a place where there is good air circulation and at room temperature, so the stock dries completely and evenly.

NOTE: If you use a quick-drying oil, such as TruOil™ or Linspeed™, dilute it 50-percent with mineral spirits or turpentine. Use an old tooth-brush to clean excess oil out of checkering, then blot gently and thoroughly with a clean, absorbent rag. If any oil remains, use a dry, soft bristled brush to brush out the oil. If you leave this kind of oil in the grooves, the checkering will fill with oil, remain sticky, attract dust, and become "dotey" so that eventually the points will wear down.

Varnished stocks

On stocks with varnish type finishes, including stocks finished with TruOil™, the above procedure can be followed, but an even better finish can be obtained with a good gunstock wax. Just follow the directions and be sure to get the excess out of the checkering.

PLASTIC AND EPOXY FINISHES

PLASTIC AND EPOXY FINISHES are best left as they are—oil will not dry on them. If you want a brighter appearance, use some stock wax.

CARE OF RECOIL PADS

DIRT AND STAINS CAN BE REMOVED from white line pads by rubbing with mineral spirits and a piece of rough cloth like denim. A strip from a worn-out pair of blue jeans works fine. Try to keep your high-intensity solvents off extra-soft recoil pads, such as Pachmayer Decelerator™ pads and Sorbocoils™. The solvents will dissolve the surface and render the pads sticky and mushy.

A metal buttplate should be treated like any other steel part. Keep it clean, brush out the checkering if necessary, and give it a thin coat of oil. Be careful that you do not get any solvent on the gunstock. Use a cotton swab to keep solvent from seeping into the seam between the wood and metal. A leather-covered pad should be treated like any other piece of leather. If it is dirty, clean it with saddle soap. If it is dry, apply neatsfoot oil. If it is dull, shoe polish will restore the color.

NOTE: Be sure to match the color of the shoe polish to the leather pad. For example, oxblood, which is a shade of brown, is different than regular brown shoe polish. If there is a scratch or gash in the leather, liquid shoe polish may discolor it to a slightly darker shade. Paste shoe polish is better and buffs to a lustrous shine.

Chapter Six

BORE OBSTRUCTIONS

As P.O. ACKLEY POINTS OUT, "The easiest way to handle the problem of an obstruction in a barrel is not to get an obstruction in it in the first place." However, problems and obstructions do occasionally happen. If you get an obstruction in the barrel of the gun you are shooting—any kind of obstruction and for any reason—you are dealing with a potentially serious problem. *The obstruction must be removed before the gun can safely be discharged again.*

Follow these steps whenever you encounter a bore obstruction. Failure to do so will result in far greater problems than that posed by the obstruction to your gun—and to you.

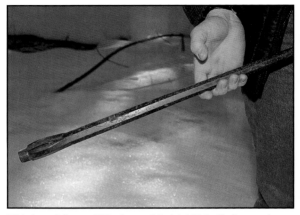

This barrel from a Winchester Model 1895 rifle burst when a cleaning patch obstructed the path of a discharged bullet. Not only was the barrel irreparably damaged—the shooter was, too.

Never shoot out an obstruction. It may result in a bulge or a burst barrel. The photograph on page 116 is an example of a ruptured barrel caused by an obstruction. In this instance, it was the barrel to a Winchester Model 95 in .38-72 caliber, a low-pressure black powder round that nevertheless was sufficient to burst the barrel. The culprit was a jammed cleaning patch that the owner tried to shoot out. Instead, he shot out his hand. A little care and some patience would have spared him this disaster. Therefore, I cannot overstress how important it is to *never attempt* to shoot out a bore obstruction. For this reason, this chapter is as comprehensive as I can make it. If it spares one person from injury or the risk of death, then consolidating my professional knowledge between the covers of this book was well worthwhile.

HOW TO REMOVE A BORE OBSTRUCTION

STEP NO. 1

Fully unload the gun

With the safety on and the muzzle pointing away from you and in a safe direction, be certain your gun is fully unloaded. This is your first priority in removing a bore obstruction. Remove all cartridges from the chamber and magazine. After you are sure, check again.

STEP NO. 2

Detach the barrel from the action

You may think this step is unnecessary. However, as the old saying goes, "It is better to be safe than sorry." Once you are certain the gun is fully unloaded, detach the barrel from the action. Handling the barrel separately will enable you to clear out the bore more easily and effectively than if you leave the barrels hanging on the gun.

STEP NO. 3

Use a cleaning-rod to try to move the obstruction

Run a cleaning-rod firmly but without force through the bore to see if the obstruction can be moved. If it can, push it out. This is best done from the muzzle; otherwise, the chokes will block the obstruction. Never force a cleaning-rod down the bore. If you do, you can jam the obstruction tighter and make removal far more difficult. If you can't move it with firm, steady pressure on the rod, then removal of the obstruction is probably a gunsmith operation that will require special tools and knowledge that the average gun owner is not likely to possess.

STEP NO. 4

Check the barrel

Shine a bore light or bright light source down the bore to make sure the obstruction is removed. It does not matter if you look down the breech or muzzle end providing the barrel is off the gun. Inspect every area of the bore by rotating the barrel slowly in your hands. Double-check to be certain no cleaning patch is left in the bore.

STEP NO. 5

Clean, Oil & Re-hang the Barrel

When you are certain the bore is completely free from any obstruction, clean the barrel inside and out. Pour hot water down the bore to remove mud. If there's time left in your hunting day, give the gun a good field cleaning then swab the bore lightly with oil before you reassemble the gun. Give it a thorough cleaning later.

PROPER REMOVAL OF BORE OBSTRUCTIONS

Caked Mud

Take a bucket of warm water and stick the muzzle of the gun in it until the mud softens. Then, using a cleaning rod and brushes, *thoroughly* remove every trace of mud. Even the thinnest residue of mud will dry and stick to the bore or outside surface of the barrel, so be sure to clean and lubricate the barrel using standard procedures.

Branches or Wooden Sticks

It is a documented fact that some shotgunners will insert a branch or stick in the bore as a means of dislodging an obstruction. There is no need to comment on the stupidity of such a performance.

However, if you are indeed guilty, there is a simple and safe way in which to resolve the situation you got yourself into, *providing the obstruction is not a cartridge*.

The 12/20 Burst

Unfortunately, the most common case of an obstruction in the field is, in fact, when a 20-gauge shell is dropped into a 12-gauge chamber or less commonly, a 28-gauge shell into a 16-gauge chamber. The cartridge drops through the chamber and lodges in the forcing cone. When a stick is used in an attempt to dislodge the shell, the result is a jammed stick *and* a live round obstructing the bore. This is a job you are definitely not qualified to deal with, and one that no gunsmith will be happy to undertake. What's more, your hunting day is over.

The following procedure was recommended by P.O. Ackley for the removal of a wooden obstruction, but can be used only on an autoloader or pump gun. Before you engage in this procedure—and I cannot repeat this often enough—be absolutely sure there is no live cartridge in the chamber. If there is, the heat will most assuredly set off the cartridge and cause it to explode. After you have removed all cartridges, then you can safely proceed.

Step One—Remove the barrel, the forend, and any sling, scope or appurtenant apparatus that may be attached to the barrel.

Step Two—Standing a safe distance from the gun, heat a propane torch to approximately 500 degrees, a temperature that is hot enough to melt solder and char the wooden obstruction. This will not injure the barrel or damage the blueing.

Step Three—Fasten the barrel in a padded vice. In the absence of such a rig, hold the uncoupled barrel with an insulated potholder. *Never* hold it with a loose rag, which can easily get in the way of the flame, and *especially* not a rag that has been used with solvents.

Step Four—Char the wooden obstruction. It will turn black and start to decompose. At that point, the branch or stick can be easily withdrawn.

Warning:

*Why you cannot perform
this procedure on a double gun.*

A 500-degree flame from a propane torch will melt the solder and loosen the ribs that join the barrels of a double gun. Of course, a stick should not have been used as a crowbar in the first place, especially on a fine gun, but if this should happen, take the gun directly to your gunsmith.

Whatever you do, *do not forget that by removing the stick, you have not removed the original obstruction*. Now you have to deal with the removal of the obstruction.

After the obstruction is removed, be sure to inspect the bore with a bore light, then clean and lubricate the barrel as usual. If you have any doubts, stop—and go to your gunsmith.

Failure to Extract

If the cartridge itself is the obstruction, pause and consider how it came to be stuck. We discussed the 12/20 burst, which applies to an unfired *live* cartridge. It is not uncommon in some guns to have a spent shell simply fail to extract and stick in the barrel after it has been fired. This could be a result of failure of the extractors, a slightly overloaded shell (which sometimes occurs in handloads, but rather more seldom in factory shells), or a rough chamber. If your gun has a tendency to regularly fail to extract a shell, see your gunsmith. It may simply be that the gun needs a good, professional cleaning.

In some model guns, a temperamental or lazy ejector can actually be a design flaw. This doesn't mean the gun is mechanically unsafe, but it will require you to carry a packable cleaning rod with you at all times so that you can manually eject the spent cartridge case whenever necessary.

When a spent cartridge is stuck in a double gun NOTE: *This procedure is not meant to dislodge a live cartridge. Don't ever monkey with a live cartridge.* A cartridge that is subjected to any kind of force can accidentally discharge—and that's a real possibility if you poke it with a cleaning rod. If the cartridge is live, then you are no longer qualified to dislodge the cartridge.

When dislodging a spent cartridge from a double gun, only perform this operation from the *muzzle* of the gun. Open your double gun. Remove the barrels, pointing them away from you and others, in a secure and safe direction. Run the cleaning rod from the muzzle end of the plugged barrel and gently poke out the spent shell. Never, under any circumstances, use an ice pick, knife blade or a steel instrument to remove the shell when working from the breech. This will almost certainly damage the chamber and cause a far worse problem than a stuck shell. If you sense you need to apply any force whatsoever to the cleaning rod, then *stop right there. Do not reassemble the gun*. Take the gun as soon as possible to a gunsmith. The problem is more than a tired or faulty ejector.

When snow and dirt get jammed in the muzzle
Remove the barrels and secure them in a padded vice. Boil water in a traditional kettle or in a pot with a lip or spout. Hold the barrel with a potholder so as not to burn your hand, then

carefully pour boiling water through the bore from the breech, standing clear of the muzzle. Ahead of time, ready a bucket in which to empty the water. This will dissolve the snow and should loosen any debris that may have settled in the bore. Check with a bore light, then clean and oil the barrel using standard procedure.

When a cleaning patch becomes lodged in the bore

There will come a time when a cleaning patch will come off the rod as you are swabbing your barrel and lodge in the bore. If it isn't lodged too tightly, you usually can push it out. If it feels snug, a few drops of oil onto the patch will help dislodge it. However, if it's really plugged in there, don't force the rod. Ideally, you will have a *worm* among your stash of cleaning rods. A *worm* is a cleaning rod with a screwhead silver-soldered to the rod. Insert the rod into the bore and twist the worm when it engages the patch. Once it strips into the cotton, it should pull out. If it fails to, insert some oil down the bore. This should loosen the patch.

If this fails, your last resort before taking it to your gunsmith may be the same process I describe for removing a wooden obstruction on page 125. Remember, *this is not a process that can be used on double guns* since the heat from the propane torch will melt the solder that couples the barrels. After you char the patch, it will come out easily with the poke of a cleaning rod. To avoid this problem in the future, be sure you thread the patch into the patch loop properly, pinging the two ends of the patch and pulling it forward from the rod.

When the rod itself becomes the obstruction

One of the most frustrating things that can exacerbate an already annoying situation is when the cleaning-rod itself lodges into the bore and becomes a *second* obstruction. When a close-fitting rod is pounded with force against a bore obstruction, the fiber of the wood can actually expand. The more you pound the rod, the more it will expand until it impacts to the point that it seems to fuse with the barrel. The propane torch procedure *will not* work in this instance. Try pouring gun oil down the barrel in hopes of freeing the rod. If that doesn't work, see your gunsmith. In dire circumstances, don't be upset if he delivers a grim prognosis. A badly impacted cleaning-rod might necessitate replacing the barrel. The way to prevent such a calamity is to only use a cleaning-rod that fits your gun, never use force when running it through the bore, and never clean a gun immediately upon bringing it into a warm room after it has been out all day in cold weather.

* * *

Although I have given you advice on how you can remove most bore obstructions, never force the issue. If an obstruction is firmly lodged, get the gun to a gunsmith as soon as possible. If you cannot unload your gun, *use every conceivable caution* to remove the barrel and get to a gunsmith. If you are concerned that an impacted, live load may fire, watch your muzzle, lock the gun away, and call your gunsmith. Never shoot out a bore obstruction under *any* circumstance!

Chapter 7

SCREWS, SCREWHEADS & TURNSCREWS

TIGHTENING AND ADJUSTING SCREWS is the only mechanical operation we will cover in this book. It is important that we discuss the subject thoroughly, for nothing is easier, quicker or more innocently performed on a gun than to "bugger" a screwhead (a gun term that means to strip the slot of a gun screw)—and nothing is more costly, "pound for pound," than replacing one.

Don't go to the local hardware store if you plan to buy screwdrivers for your gun. You will not find the type you need to properly tighten and adjust gun screws. Common-variety screwdrivers are intended for carpentry use, not for gun work. Ordinary steel is not sufficiently hardened for gun screws, and the taper makes it difficult to keep the tip in position. Gun screw slots are small. They measure from .025 to .057-inch. If you use an inappropriate screwdriver, the taper will raise burs on the screwhead and possibly strip the slot. You need screwdrivers specifically made for gun work. *Nothing else will do.*

A properly fitted tip of a gun screwdriver will not come out of the slot and will not damage the screwhead. A damaged or distorted screwhead will result from a bit that does not fit the slot in every dimension—damage that is unthinkable in a fine gun and undesirable in any gun. If a screw is badly buggered and needs to be replaced, you are looking at an extensive search to find a replacement if the gun is no longer made, and a very expensive proposition if a new one has to be made— especially if it involves engraving. Frequently you can get replacement screws from the manufacturer if the gun is still in production, but even then, it can be a frustrating and time-intensive ordeal.

The best solution to any potential problem is the preventative approach. Therefore, do not even consider adjusting a gun screw without the proper screwdriver. You'll regret it, I assure you.

Not all gun screws are the same

There is an important difference between the design of the slot of screwheads in American and most production guns, versus the slot of British "best" and fine continental guns. Specific screwdrivers are required for each.

The *square slotted screw* is found in American guns and most production guns manufactured the world over. This screw has a machine-cut, flat bottomed slot with parallel sides. Even the best quality American guns, as far as I know, are square slotted. The proper tools for square slotted screws are hollow-ground screwdrivers. A hollow-ground screwdriver is "scooped" so the sides of the tip are parallel to fit the slot of the screw precisely. This is called an *ogive cut*. In a typical, square-slotted screw, this enables the screwdriver bit to contact the entire screw slot without risk of casting up burs on the edges or distorting the screwhead in any way. Hollow-ground screwdrivers are available through gunsmithing supply houses. These are easily modified to fit any particular slot by using simple grinding techniques.

"V" slotted screws are found on most handmade British and continental guns. The slots are most often cut with special "V" shaped files. Special screwdrivers called *turnscrews* must be made to fit a "V" slotted screw. Because the slots are handmade, there is no standard "V" cut. However, those drivers supplied with a gun or fitted in deluxe gun-cleaning kits are specifically meant for these screws. If you use a hollow ground screwdriver in a "V" slot, you are sure to tear out the edges of the slot. Conversely, if you use a "V" slotted turnscrew in a square-slotted screw, you will distort the edges of *that* slot. Proper turnscrews for "V" slotted screws are not commonly available in the United States. In Europe, a custom gunmaker makes his own turnscrews. Each is designed to fit a particular type of screw for the gun he is making.

North-South Alignment

All fine European guns and better American guns have the screw slots aligned North-South, or in a direct line from butt to muzzle. The reason is *not* purely aesthetics. When a screw slot is positioned North-South and flush with the surrounding metal, it means the screw is properly aligned and fully tightened. However, be careful: *Do not overtighten a screwhead past this position.* If you venture to overtighten a screw, you run the risk of twisting the head right off the shank and then you have a very serious problem that can only be rectified by a professional gunsmith. On production guns, American or European notwithstanding, it may be difficult to get a screw to line up North-South using a screwdriver. If you cannot move it by hand, the screw was probably put in by a drill press. In this instance, leave it alone and consult a professional gunsmith.

In most production shotguns, the screwheads are not lined up, such as the Winchester Model 12, Ithaca Model 37, Remington Model 1100 (which does not have many screws, anyway), Beretta and Benelli automatic shotguns, Mossberg 500, and most domestic and import slide-actions and semi-automatic shotguns. In these model guns, tighten the screws with moderate manual pressure until the screw won't move further under regular and consistent pressure. If they tend to loosen, use a drop of Loc-Tite® or other thread-locking compound directly onto the threads. This locks the screw in place, though it can be removed with firm pressure if desired. If the screw does not move, use a little heat from a hairdryer. The heat will break the bond, and you can back the screw out.

How to properly tighten a loose gun screw

1. Secure the gun in a gun cradle. Be sure you have the appropriate screwdriver for the screwhead. To position the tip of the screwdriver into the screwhead, hold the screwdriver firmly in a vertical position and lower the tip into the slot.

2. Hold the tip of the screwdriver in the fingers of one hand and turn the handle with the fingers of the other hand. All screws (with the exception of left-hand threaded screws) turn in a clockwise direction. With gentle and consistent pressure, turn the screwdriver until it stops moving, making sure that the tip of the screwdriver remains in full contact and square to the head of the screw.

3. When the screw stops moving under light pressure, grasp the handle of the screwdriver and give it one more firm turn to lock it in place. That will prevent it from coming out under normal use. Don't force the screw any further than it will go and never past North-South alignment, if that is the way the gun was made.

Some helpful hints about gun screws

Popular production guns, such as the Winchester Model 12, are notorious for screws that tend to loosen from the force of recoil. The screws can easily fall out and become lost during use. This is especially true of the screws located at the forward end of the magazine tube that attach the magazine tube bracket to the barrel. Such screws are best mounted with a thread-locking compound to prevent "backing out." Other than that, the procedure is the same as above.

Whenever you have a screw mounted close to the barrel, you must assume that it is likely to loosen under the shock of firing. If it becomes loose, it should be reinforced with a thread-locking compound, such as Lock-Tite® or Lock-It®.

Always check the screws on your gun visually every time you clean it.

Check each screw manually at the end of the season; more frequently, if the gun sees heavy use.

Removing a tightly embedded screw is a job that is best left for a professional gunsmith. A few seconds of unrequited frustration on your part can leave an unsightly scar on your gun. Many a temper tantrum has led to tearing off a screw slot, distorting or damaging the screwhead, or worse. In these instances, all you can do is calm down, learn from your mistake—and get out your checkbook because, in all probability, you're going to have to pay for your impatience with a visit to the gunsmith.

The ultimate horror story is a buggered *engraved* screw. This was the case on a pre-War Francotte side-by-side I acquired. Two of the screwheads had been so badly damaged that the engraving was destroyed and it was impossible to get a screwdriver bit in the slot. In a case like this, a professional gunsmith will have to weld up the screwhead with a Tig welder, then turn it down with a lathe to the proper height, recut the slot with a slitting saw, then have the screw re-engraved by a firearms engraver. Cost? Suffice it say, you could buy a good, used pump gun for the same money.

If you shoot a double gun that has an enclosed action, you may experience difficulty closing the gun. Do not force it to close! Chances are the ejector retaining screw (located on the barrel lumps) is loose. If it is not flush to the metal, then it needs to be tightened and for this you must use the appropriate turnscrew. You can do this operation, providing you use the right tool and do not force the screw. If you are uncertain, take the gun to your gunsmith. It is common for this particular screw to become loose, since the lumps are constantly subject to the force of recoil.

Tang screws also tend to loosen. The lower tang is where the trigger guard bends into the grip and the upper tang is where the safety is generally located. Usually the tang screw can only be reached by removing the trigger guard. Over-tightening or loosening it can change the pressure of the triggers against the sears and cause double firing (or no firing at all), or can prevent the safety from working. Unless you are familiar with this operation, see your professional gunsmith.

You may notice that the wood-to-metal fit on a draw bolt gun isn't tight. This is a common problem on the Winchester Model 12, and Remington models 870 and 1100—in fact, most pump guns and semi-automatic shotguns. If the wood gets dry, the gunstock will shrink and pull away from the action. Sometimes firing causes further damage and in the worst case scenario, can even cause the stock to crack. That's because the stock is slamming into the receiver every time it is fired. To tighten the draw bolt, remove the buttplate. Using a large-headed screwdriver, tighten the bolt. This is the only instance I can think of when you can safely use a hardware store variety screwdriver. Turn the bolt until it no longer moves. Do not over-tighten, as you can damage the stock. Sometimes the screw threads of a bolt do not go deep enough to draw up the stock. This can be cured, but it is a gunsmith operation. If tightening the draw bolt does not solve the problem, the stock may need to be rebedded. If the shrinkage is significant, it may be best to get a new replacement stock, available through the manufacturer or mail-order houses such as Brownells. Consult your gunsmith.

Chapter 8

TRAVELING WITH YOUR GUN

ALTHOUGH MOST WINGSHOOTING LODGES AND SPORTING CLAYS CLUBS have gun-cleaning facilities, it is always a good idea to be prepared. A portable travel kit such as the one pictured on page 53 is easy to pack. However, if you are going on a hunting trip, you need to be prepared for any circumstance.

As we discussed, the best travel rod is a jointed aluminum rod. It's lightweight and easy to pack—along with gun patches, powder solvent, lubricating oil and silicone cloths for wiping down the stock and barrels. Hoppe's Universal Field Cleaning Kit is a neat little rig that comes in a soft pack that hooks onto your belt and includes a six-piece aluminum rod. A jointed rod serves as a useful tool in dislodging most bore obstructions or removing a spent shell when the extractors or ejectors fail—something a pull-through cannot do. If you are hunting ducks, it is a good idea to tote along a can of rust preventative or an all-around solvent such as Young's "303" Oil, a time-honored barrel cleaner, rust preventative and lubricant. This will displace moisture, retard rust, and oil your gun. Rust, as all duck hunters know, appears like lightening when gunmetal is exposed to saltwater or salt-laden air, as in marshes or along the seashore. One thing many shotgunners fail to bring along is a supply of thirsty, clean cotton rags. These are indispensable, especially if your gun is subjected to inclement weather or accidentally submerged.

Chapter 9

How to Find a
Professional Gunsmith

UP TO THIS POINT, I have guided you to the best of
my ability in the ways and methods that will
successfully enable you to properly maintain and
care for your gun under normal (and a few
abnormal) conditions. As I have repeatedly stated,
past a certain point it is advisable to stop and
surrender your gun to the care of a professional
gunsmith. As I say in the Appendix which bears
repeating, *gunsmiths are made, not born. If you don't
know, don't try.* You may not believe me now, but
you will if you attempt to do work that you are not
qualified to undertake.

It is not difficult to find a gunsmith, although it isn't easy to find a competent one who specializes in fine shotgun work. They're out there, but these professionals are few and far between. A good source is *Black's Wing & Clay*. Ask your gun dealer, local sporting goods store, and shooting partners who they recommend *based on personal experience*. "I hear that so-and-so is pretty good" just doesn't cut it. The relationship between a gunsmith and his client is, for some sportsmen, akin to their relationship with their doctor, stockbroker or lawyer. You need to have confidence in your gunsmith's judgment and ability, and ideally establish a good, long-term rapport with him. You want someone who you are comfortable conferring with and will visit repeatedly, season after season. Your gunsmith will come to know your guns and your eccentricities as a sportsman just as your doctor knows your blood pressure and general physical health.

Never "stop in" to see a gunsmith without an appointment. If he doesn't know you from Adam, you are under a misunderstanding if you think that he'll be thrilled to see you. If you are a regular client, he may be happy to see you, but if he's engulfed in work, your visit may not be welcome. Say he's in the middle of blueing—a dangerous and precisely timed operation—or has disassembled a sidelock. Don't be offended if he turns you out or doesn't even answer the door. Would you interrupt your doctor in the middle of an operation? A gunsmith is no different. He's doing his job. Just like anyone who charges for professional services, "time is money." Most gunsmith shops are one-man operations. If you want to meet a gunsmith, call in advance and make an appointment. When you make an appointment, ask if there is a charge for his time, whether you leave a gun with him to work on or not. This way you will know what to expect, and he'll appreciate the courtesy.

When you meet a gunsmith for the first time, ask him where he received his training. How many years has he been practicing his trade? What is his specialty? Does he work on the type of gun you have? Does he price by the job or by the hour? Does he give written estimates and guarantee costs within 10-percent either way of that estimate? What is his turnaround time on a standard job? Is there a specific job you need now or soon, such as lengthening or cutting a stock, reboring a barrel, etc., which he can—or can not—do? Will he supply you with personal references? These are all good questions. Ask them.

Chapter 10

HELPFUL HINTS FROM THE
GUNSMITH'S BENCH

*Here are some useful tips that will help you at the
bench and in the field . . .*

☐ WHEN HUNTING IN HEAVY RAIN OR SNOW, a
piece of plastic wrap placed snugly over the muzzles
will keep the bore dry.

☐ When oiling trigger groups and other small parts
or areas in the action, dip the point of a lead pencil
into a jar of gun oil and use it to place a small drop
exactly where needed.

☐ Put a "ring" of oil on your wool mop. This will enable you to clean and oil in one pass without over-oiling.

☐ Carry a jointed cleaning rod at all times. Not only can you use this to clean your gun in the field, marsh or on the range, but it can also be used to dislodge crusted snow or other bore obstructions. Some model shotguns are notorious for having lazy ejectors. If this is the case, the rod can be pushed down the muzzle to eject the hull.

☐ *Alcohol and gunpowder don't mix.* Keep the liquor off the field, the range and out of the gun room.

☐ Extreme humidity can raise Cain with your gun's functioning—but it may well resume normal operation when allowed to dry. Just make sure it's dry and oiled before you put it away.

☐ Gunsmiths are made, not born. If you don't know, don't try.

☐ Old, gummy oil is a natural magnet for airborne dust. Keep it clean!

☐ Penetrating solvents can deactivate primers. Wipe the bore and chamber dry before use.

☐ Aerosol oils contain an extremely volatile propellant. If used too close to the gun's surface, it can blow off the surface oil and then evaporate, leaving gunmetal clean, dry—and subject to condensation and rust. Back off about 6–8 inches when spraying aerosol oils.

☐ Trigger groups of pump guns and semi-automatics should be removed and thoroughly cleaned once or twice a year, depending on how heavily the gun is used. Disassembly is not required but cleaning is, in order to prevent jams from accumulated fouling.

☐ Double guns are designed to be closed smartly, allowing the top lever to snap gently into place. Do not close the gun slowly and ease the top lever into place as this may result in the failure of the action to lock properly.

☐ If a gas-operated shotgun, especially one with an aluminum receiver, begins to operate unreliably, the trouble may not be dirt. If the gun has been heavily used, the rails may be worn past maximum tolerance. Nothing can be done about this, even by the factory. It's time for a new gun.

☐ Under the sun, all things wear to an end at last—guns as well as people. If Grandpa's old Fox will not work well despite repeated trips to the gunsmith, maybe it's time to place it on the wall in honorable retirement. After 70 or 80 years of hard service, the gun owes you nothing. Would that we could all perform as well!

☐ All oils dry eventually—except one. That one is the one you can't get anymore: sperm oil, from the endangered sperm whale. Brownell's sold this until the early 1970s by the half-pint can. If you can find some, use it like liquid gold. It's wonderful, but there will be no more.

☐ Don't use a metal scraper to remove accumulated gunk. Soak parts in one of the high-intensity bore cleaners for 24- to 48-hours, then scrub clean with a phosphor bronze utility brush. Repeat if necessary.

☐ The recoil spring on the Browning A5, Remington Model 11, and other long-recoil operated shotguns must be properly lubricated for optimum function. Use a plain, petroleum-based oil in liquid form. Aerosol products are too volatile. Apply a sufficient amount of oil and make sure it gets into the magazine tube—here is one place where you will need a thorough coating. Wipe off the excess with a soft cloth. Work the action back and forth several times.

☐ Keep oily rags in a sealed container to avoid the risk of spontaneous combustion.

☐ On repeating shotguns with tubular magazines, do not attempt to remove the magazine spring retainer. It is under heavy spring tension, easily lost, and difficult to get back in. A squirt of good aerosol gun lube will be enough for all but the dirtiest tube, and if it gets that bad, it should go to the gunsmith.

☐ To reassemble some double barreled shotguns, it is necessary to hold the top lever over to the right.

☐ Forends on double guns should be seated home with a firm tap from the heel of the palm to ensure complete locking.

☐ When cleaning doubles, do not forget to lubricate both the locking bolt in the action and the locking surface on the barrel lugs. A small quantity of light grease is best. Same for the forend latch and lug.

☐ If you have a matched pair or set of guns, or are shooting a popular make and model gun at a gun club, check to be certain that the serial number on the barrels matches the serial number on the stock when you put the gun back together. This kind of undesirable mix-up does happen, and this simple check will save you a lot of aggravation.

☐ If you are on a hunting trip in cold weather, do not leave your gun in the car overnight. Condensation can form in the barrels, freeze and *become a bore obstruction.* If your gun is left in the cold for a prolonged period, bring it inside and allow the barrels to warm up. To be certain no frozen condensation remains, run a warm, moist patch through the bores. If significant ice has formed, remove the barrels, allow the barrels to warm to room temperature, then run boiling water through the bores. In either case, give the bores a final pass with a fresh patch and a drop or two of gun oil or lubricant before you re-hang the barrels. This frequently happens with duck guns. Remember, cold does not prevent rust—and nothing is more insidious in causing rust than saltwater and salt-laden air.

A Well-Stocked Workbench

Chapter 11

How to Build a Workbench

An ordinary table will not serve as a suitable work surface for cleaning your guns. It is not sturdy enough and usually too low to work at while standing. However, a proper bench can be made with minimal time and expense from commonly available lumber.

Specifications for 6 x 3-foot workbench,
approximately 37-inches high

Materials

Four 4 x 4-inch timbers, 36-inches long

Four 2 x 8-inch boards, 36-inches long

Two 2 x 8-inch boards, 72-inches long

One 4 x 8-foot sheet of interior finish
plywood, 3/4-inches thick

16-d (penny) nails

6-d nails

Tools

Hammer

Crosscut saw (hand or power)

Tape measure (at least 8-foot)

Carpenter's square

Procedure

It is difficult to cut heavy timbers accurately by hand so that they are truly square. This applies especially to 4 x 4 timbers. It would be best to have the timbers cut to length at the lumber yard, which can usually be done for a modest fee—and will allow you to start with pieces that are cut just as they should be.

Using 6-d nails, attach one of the six foot 2 x 8 boards to one end of each of two 4 x 4 timbers. Use your square to make sure the legs are vertical. Attach so that the end of the 4 x 4 is level with the top edge of the 2 x 8, and the sawn edges of the 2 x 8 are flush with the outside edge of the 4 x 4 timbers. Use at least six nails to secure at each end. Repeat the procedure with the other two 4 x 4s and the remaining six-foot 2 x 8. This will give you the two outer panels of the bench. Attach a three-foot 2 x 8 to the end, flush with the outer edge of the 2 x 8 boards and use your square to mark a vertical line. Take the two remaining three-foot 2 x 8 boards and attach at these points. It should be a snug fit. Use three 16-d nails for each.

Turn the assembled bench upright. Lay the piece of plywood on the top. Line up one edge of the plywood with the long side of the bench and another with the short side, and tack in place with a few 6-d nails—*do not pound them in all the way.*

Using a pencil, mark the other two edges of the bench on the underside of the plywood. Remove the temporary nails and turn the plywood over. Use your crosscut saw to saw out the traced outline of the bench. This will be the bench top. Attach it securely to the bench support with 6-d nails—plenty of them! Make sure that the finish side of the plywood is uppermost. Stain and finish the top surface with two coats of urethane varnish—spray type is the easiest.

You now have a heavy, sturdy bench that is high enough to work at easily while standing.

* * *

APPENDIX

Products featured in this book

THE ORVIS COMPANY

Historic Route 7A

Manchester, VT 05254-0798

To order this book or Orvis products depicted in this book, or to request a catalogue call 1-800-548-9548

HOLLAND & HOLLAND 50 East 57th St., NY, NY 10022

GALAZAN, P. O. Box 1692, New Britain, CT 06051

BROWNELLS, 200 South Front St., Montezuma, IA 50171

HOPPE'S, Airport Industrial Mall, Coatesville, PA 19320

BIRCHWOOD CASEY, Fuller Rd, EdenPrairie, MN 55344

J. DEWEY, P. O. Box 2104, Southbury, CT 06488

MS. MOLY ™, 1966 Knob Road, Burlington, WI 53105

BREAK-FREE, 1035 South Linwood, Santa Ana, CA 92705

CHEM-PAK, P.O. Box 2058, Winchester VA 22604

LPS LABORATORIES, P. O. Box 5052, Tucker, GA 30085

KLEEN-BORE, 16 Industrial Pky, Easthampton, MA 01027

FLITZ International, 821 Mohr Ave, Waterford, WI 53185

IOSSO Products, 1485 Lively Blvd., Elk Grove, IL 60007

CHOKE SHINE, Rte. 2, Box 31,Collins, GA 30421

THE ORVIS GUNSMITHING DEPARTMENT

I wish to thank the master gunsmiths of the Orvis Gunsmithing Department for their collaboration with this book. They offer a full-service shop that specializes in shotgun repairs, stockmaking, engraving, and custom gunmaking. For inquiries, call (802) 362-7055, fax (802) 362-0480.

INDEX